YOUTH MINISTRY
QUESTIONS

Lessons from a Life-Long Youth Worker

MEL WALKER

WESTBOW
P R E S S®
A DIVISION OF THOMAS NELSON
& ZONDERVAN

WestBow Press books may be ordered through booksellers or by contacting:

WestBow Press
A Division of Thomas Nelson & Zondervan
1663 Liberty Drive
Bloomington, IN 47403
www.westbowpress.com
844-714-3454

ISBN: 978-1-6642-6571-4 (sc)
ISBN: 978-1-6642-6570-7 (e)

Print information available on the last page.

WestBow Press rev. date: 5/9/2022

TABLE OF CONTENTS

Section 2: Reaching and Ministering to Emerging Generations

Section 3: Parents and Households of Teenagers

Section 4: Utilizing Other Youth Workers

Section 5: Youth Ministry Connections

Section 6: Ministering to Your Church's Young Adults

Section 7: Other Important Youth Ministry Topics

DEDICATION

This book is dedicated to my former youth ministry students. I know that your impact upon the next generation will far exceed mine.

> *"To Him be glory in the church by Christ Jesus to all generations, forever and ever. Amen."*
> Ephesians 3:21

INTRODUCTION AND PREFACE

What qualified Mel Walker to write a book providing answers to youth ministry questions? Was he truly an expert on the topic?

Mel was my dad, and what you might call a youth ministry "lifer". He began his career in youth ministry at Calvary Baptist Church in Ypsilanti, Michigan in the late 1970s and ministered to the next generation until he passed away on December 2, 2021 (two weeks after this book was due to be submitted to the publisher). He devoted over 45 years to reaching the next generation and training others to do the same.

It's a rare thing for someone to be in youth ministry for 45 years. Many only stay in the position for a few years. But youth ministry wasn't just a job for my dad; his life's passion was "that the generation to come might know" (Psalm 78:6, NKJV). He served as a youth pastor, mentor, youth ministry professor at two separate Bible colleges, youth curriculum writer and editor, director of a leadership conference for teenagers, worked with colleagues to start a National Youth Ministries Conference, co-founded Vision For Youth, an international network for youth ministry, and authored more than a dozen books on youth ministry, mentoring, and connecting the generations.

The above resume points to a true expert in the field, in my opinion, but don't take my word for it. Read the book and see what you think.

I couldn't be more proud of my dad or more privileged to have had a front row seat for over 43 of his 45+ years in youth ministry. I learned so much that I myself went into youth ministry, serving as the Director of Student Ministries at an international church in Berlin, Germany for 17 years. Mel's passion was truly contagious.

May God bless you as you learn from someone who gave his life to see the next generation go on for God.

Kristi Walker

SECTION 1

Youth Ministry Basics

CHAPTER 1

IS YOUTH MINISTRY BIBLICAL?

A DEBATE IS OCCURRING IN SOME Christian circles about a perceived lack of a Biblical basis for youth ministry. Some voices are blaming youth work for the much-reported departure of young adults from the church following high school.[1] Others are seeming to simply deemphasize youth ministry in lieu of other church programs such as worship and the weekend services where all age groups gather in the church auditorium.

Proponents of the anti-youth ministry movement contend that there is no support in the Bible for an age-divided church.[2] These voices argue that because churches have historically segregated the various generations into ministry silos (including children's ministry, young ministry, and college-age ministry to list some examples), there is a lack of cross-generational connections in the church which has resulted in a mass exodus of emerging adults from the church.

The Next Generation Principle in Scripture

However, interwoven throughout the narrative of Scripture is a rather obvious principle. Each generation is expected to reproduce their faith in the lives of the succeeding generation. There are numerous illustrations of this "next generation principle" in the Bible. Here are a few examples.

1. *Moses' ministry in the life of Joshua*

The story of Moses is certainly one of the most compelling leadership accounts in the Bible. Moses may have been one of the greatest leaders the world has ever known. Yet, he was a man with all-too-human flaws and weaknesses, one of which became the "Achilles Heel" that kept him from entering the promised land (Deuteronomy 32:51-52).

One of Moses' greatest accomplishments may have been his positive response to God's instruction to train Joshua to be his successor as the next leader of Israel (Numbers 27:12-23). The Old Testament narrative describes how Moses willingly trained young Joshua to lead during the next stage of Israel's history. This story is a great illustration of how God wanted His people to reproduce their faith in the lives of the next generation.

The full narrative of the nation of Israel also contains a negative example of how Joshua personally failed in his own implementation of what Moses had taught him about leadership. The account is found in Judges 2:7-10. God's Word makes a point to tell readers that "the people served the Lord all the days of Joshua, and all the days of the elders who outlived Joshua." But the story takes a disappointing turn in verse 10, "When all that generation had been gathered to their fathers, another generation arose after them who did not know the Lord nor the work which He has done for Israel." Joshua failed to do what Moses had done with him. He did not invest his life in someone younger to take his place.

2. *God's command to Israel in Deuteronomy 6*

Another example of this principle is found in the familiar account of God's clear instruction to Israel in Deuteronomy 6. In this passage, the Word of God emphasizes the Shema, a twice-daily prayer that helped the Jewish people understand and remember the role that their relationship with God should have in their lives.[3] "Hear O Israel: The Lord our God, the Lord is one! You shall love the Lord your God will all your heart, with all your soul, and with all your strength" (verses 4 and 5).

Obviously, the main focus of this chapter is for parents, especially fathers (verse 2), to teach these words "diligently" to their children (verse 6) as life happened. Godly parents were expected to make their love for God such a priority that it would permeate every aspect of their lives. That life itself should be considered as a teaching opportunity to communicate these truths to their children.

There is one other emphasis in Deuteronomy 6 that deserves attention. Notice that this chapter (verses 3 and 4, "Hear, O Israel"), and the entire book of Deuteronomy (Deuteronomy 1:1, "These are the words which Moses spoke to all Israel...") is written to the nation of Israel as a whole. Youth pastor and author, Mike McGarry, makes an important point in his book, *A Biblical Theology of Youth Ministry*: "Parents were given the primary calling to impress the commands of Scripture on their children's minds and hearts, but this was never meant for parents alone... All the generations of Israel were expected to come together in order to raise up the younger generations for covenantal faithfulness."[4]

The Jewish people were obviously a part of a community of what God was doing. Parents were never expected to carry the total burden of teaching and training their children alone. The entire community was actively involved in the process of communicating God's truth to the next generation.

3. *Elijah's ministry in the life of Elisha*

Another Old Testament example of this principle is found in the story of Elijah and his successor, Elisha. 1 Kings 19 gives the account of God telling Elijah to "anoint" Elisha to be a prophet in his place (1 Kings 19:16).

There is a very revealing statement in verse 21 of that chapter. "(Elisha)… followed Elijah, and became his servant." Elisha was expected to learn from Elijah by staying close to him and by watching how Elijah lived and ministered. Elijah obeyed the Lord and committed himself to train someone younger who could carry on his work after he was taken by the Lord up into heaven (2 Kings 2:11).

4. *Christ's ministry with His disciples*

Christ Himself also vividly demonstrated this principle in His ministry with His disciples. There is Biblical evidence that suggests that the majority of Jesus' followers were young men at the time of His training ministry with them. There may have been only two of His disciples who were "grownups" at the time. One would be the Apostle Peter, whom the Bible tells us was married (Matthew 8:14-15). The other would be Matthew, otherwise known as Levi, who was already employed as a "tax collector" (Matthew 9:9-12) when he was called to follow Jesus.

It is obvious from reading the Gospels that Jesus focused His earthly ministry on training the next generation. He called them to walk away from their families (Matthew 4:18-22, Luke 5:1-11, Luke 14:26) to be discipled by someone other than their parents. This group of students were mostly young men who were called and trained by Christ to carry on His ministry on Earth after He returned to heaven.

5. *Paul's ministry with younger men*

The Bible also contains several examples of how the Apostle Paul invested his life in the lives of younger men. Two notable examples jump out of the pages of the New Testament. The first was John Mark who was obviously a young man when he was chosen to accompany Paul (and Barnabas) on the very first mission trip ever. (This account is found in Acts 12 -13).) The other was Timothy, a young man from a humanly dysfunctional family, who was also recruited by the Apostle to go along with him on another missionary endeavor. (This story is located in Acts 16:1-8.) These two young men are introduced in Scripture alongside their parents, and yet they too were discipled by someone else. In this case, by the Apostle Paul.

It's interesting to also note in Scripture that Paul expected his disciples to keep this pattern of discipling the next generation going. 2 Timothy 2:2 puts it this way: "...the things that you have heard from me among many witnesses, commit these to faithful men who will be able to teach others also." In this letter Paul made his instructions quite clear. Timothy was to invest his life in the lives of the next generation and to intentionally train other younger men to carry on this strategy as well.

Other Biblical Principles to Consider

The Bible also contains some important educational principles that apply to this question. Passages such as 1 Corinthians 13:11 ("When I was a child, I spoke as a child, I understood as a child, I thought as a child; but when I became a man, I put away childish things") give credence to an age-segregated teaching ministry. It only makes sense to realize that children learn at a different level than do adults.

Other key passage that provides important instruction for church ministries is Ephesians 4:14-16, which says, "that we should no longer be children, tossed to and fro and carried about by every wind of doctrine, by the trickery of men, in the cunning craftiness of deceitful plotting, but, speaking the truth in love, may grow up in all things into the head–Christ."

It's clear from this text that the church has a Biblical responsibility to help children "grow up" spiritually by providing instruction from called and qualified pastors and teachers (verse 11).

Later in this same epistle, the Apostle Paul turns his attention to parents, especially fathers, by challenging them to "bring up" their own children in the "training and admonition of the Lord" (Ephesians 6:4). These two God-ordained institutions (the church and Christian parents) are to be actively involved in the process of helping children grow in spiritual maturity. Here too, the vitally important process of raising children for the Lord was never intended to fall on parents only. The New Testament presents the training functions that a community of believers in the local church can have as well.

Practical Applications for Today

The Bible clearly presents this important next generation principle. Each generation is expected to reproduce their faith in the lives of future generations. Of course, this mandate applies to Christian parents who have the primary responsibility of raising children to grow up in spiritual maturity.

However, parents in Scripture were not expected to shoulder this responsibility all alone. Believers have historically been a part of a community of other Godly people, some of whom have the God-given calling and privilege to teach and disciple the next generation to actively live for the Lord and to serve Him.

Christian parents must take their responsibility to raise their children "in the training and admonition of the Lord" (Ephesians 6:4) very seriously, but they do not have to do it by themselves. God's community today, the local church, has other Godly adults who can be used by God to assist in the discipling process of the next generation. That's what youth ministry is all about.

CHAPTER 2

DOES OUR YOUTH MINISTRY WORK?

YOUTH MINISTRY MAY BE GETTING a bad rap.

The drop-out statistics are well documented and much reported. Young adults are leaving the church,[1] or are not making the church a priority;[2] and a variety of voices in evangelical Christianity are blaming church youth ministry for this departure.

But what if the problem actually rests with "big church"? Maybe today's students love and profit greatly from youth ministry, and because the church as a whole is nothing like the youth ministry, the kids feel like they don't belong, and therefore walk away looking for something else.

Maybe youth ministry has it right. Let's not forget that most people accept Christ, and many make lifetime spiritual decisions when they are young.[3] Teenagers go on more short-term missions trips than adults.[4] More Christian teens share their faith than do Christian adults.[5]

Perhaps churches should operate more like youth ministries. This may sound somewhat factious and controversial, but maybe if lead pastors would run their churches like youth pastors run their youth groups, there might be more growing churches.

What if youth ministry is doing things correctly? In fact, maybe the church as a whole should adopt and embrace the many positive aspects of youth ministry. The constructive characteristics of youth ministry may be the exact things that would help keep them in church as young adults.

Please don't dismiss this premise without thinking it through! The problem of emerging adults leaving the church following high school is serious enough that this issue should be carefully examined from all viewpoints and not just assume that youth ministry must be at fault. A God-honoring, Biblically-based, and culturally-relevant initiative like youth ministry must not be dismissed due to a prejudicial hypothesis or because of an over-reaction to negative statistics. A careful and historical look at the discipline of youth ministry will reveal some life-long, positive, and God-honoring results in the lives of countless people.

There are, of course, significant weaknesses in some local church youth programs. Some use entertainment to attract teenagers, other youth programs use activities to keep teens busy, others provide programming the teens themselves have selected, while others try to build their youth programs upon the strong personalities of extroverted adult youth "experts".

Before unilaterally accepting the premise that youth ministry is failing, churches should take a careful look at the kind of youth ministry that is "working" and that is producing Godly high school graduates who greatly desire to go on for Christ as adults.

Why Youth Ministry Should Be a Priority

There are at least five significant reasons why youth ministry should be a top priority in the church.

1. *Christian teens need in-depth and life-related teaching of the Scriptures.*

    The hallmark of local church youth ministry must be its focus on the thorough and creative teaching of the Word of God. Today's young people are growing up with tough questions about a variety of life's issues, and they need to know where to go for the answers. They can find entertainment and activities in other places. This does not mean that churches should never host functions that are fun or imaginative. But church youth ministry must be characterized by the clear presentation of the Gospel.

    Youth workers must also teach the Scriptures so that teenagers see that there are Biblical principles that apply to their lives today. The Apostle Paul's instruction in 2 Timothy 3:16-17 ("All Scripture is given by inspiration of God, and is profitable for doctrine, for reproof, for correction, for instruction in righteousness, that the man of God may be complete, thoroughly equipped for every good work.") is an important passage that highlights the importance of teaching the Word of God in a way that impacts specific areas of life.

2. *Christian teens need fellowship with other Christian teenagers.*

    Interaction with peers is very important for this age group. One veteran youth worker put it this way, "Friends are the very lifeblood of adolescence."[6] Church youth ministry must be a place where Christian young people can connect with other Christian teens. Most readers will remember the story of Shadrach, Meshach, and Abednego in Daniel 3. One of the most interesting aspects of that story is that these three Israeli captives are always mentioned together. Undoubtedly it was easier for them to take this life-threatening stand for God because they did it together. The same principle applies to young people today. Godly young people need to know that there are other Christian teenagers who love the Lord and who are willing to take a stand for Him. Church youth ministry is the place where that is most likely to happen.

3. *Christian teens need Godly inter-generational connections.*

Another key aspect of local church youth ministry is the opportunity teens have there to connect with believers from other generations. Young people especially need a variety of adult mentors. This is the principle that the Apostle Paul shared in Titus 2:1-8, where he instructed older, more mature believers to mentor younger believers in practical areas of their lives. It's a shame if local churches isolate teenagers almost exclusively from other generations. A variety of Godly older adults can serve as spiritual mentors to young people in the church. Wise youth workers should be intentional about providing opportunities for teenagers to develop healthy and growing relationships with Godly older people in the church. Likewise, youth workers should provide ways for teenagers to serve the Lord in the church's ministry to children as well, giving them ways to connect with other generations in the church.

4. *Christian teens need outlets for service and outreach.*

Church is also the place for teens to experience both ministry and evangelistic opportunities. Christian young people need encouraging and safe places where they can utilize their spiritual gifts in significant ways. The description of the church in Ephesians 4:11-16 presents the idea that God's church only functions correctly when everyone is doing their part. We must not tell younger generations to grow up before they can serve. Churches should be proactive about providing ways for young people to serve the Lord as they grow towards spiritual maturity. Christian teens also need opportunities to share their faith in Christ with others. Church youth ministry should provide an environment for them to learn how to present the Gospel, and they should arrange occasions to do just that.

5. *Christian teens need to develop lifelong spiritual disciplines.*

The local church should work alongside of Christian parents to build lasting habits of spiritual disciplines into the lives of young people. Passages like Ephesians 6:4 and Ephesians 4:14-15 teach the importance of both God-ordained institutions (the family and the church) being integrally involved in the training of young people in their growth toward lasting spiritual maturity. Spiritual disciplines like Scripture memory, a consistent prayer life, giving, serving, and even regularly attending church must be implemented into the fabrics of both Christian homes and local church programming. This reinforcement of both the home and the church working together will help produce lasting habits in the lives of children and young people that are more likely to be practiced throughout their lives.

These five reasons build a case for the importance of local church youth ministry. The teaching of God's Word, fellowship with other believers, inter-generational mentoring, service and evangelism, as well as the implementation of spiritual disciplines must be essential ingredients of any church's youth ministry. These are the very things that can keep youth ministry from getting a bad rap and that can help young people grow up toward Spiritual maturity.

CHAPTER 3

WHY WOULD TEENAGERS WALK AWAY FROM CHURCH FOLLOWING ACTIVE INVOLVEMENT IN YOUTH GROUP?

ACCORDING TO RECENT SURVEYS ALMOST 70% of high school graduates quit going to church during their college-age years.[1] As I mentioned in the previous two chapters, a common reaction is to blame youth ministry. The arguments are something like this:

- "the youth group is entertainment-based",
- "it separates generations", and
- "it replaces parents as the primary influencers over young people."

It's easy to blame the youth program. But I wonder...

Of course, the root of this situation certainly lies within the family. Parents are the primary influence over their children even as the kids age into their late teenage years. But as I also asked in an earlier chapter, what if the problem is with "big church"? Maybe today's students love and profit greatly from youth ministry; and because the adult ministries of the church are nothing like the youth ministry, the kids feel as if they don't fit and therefore leave the church.

I must admit, however, that I have seen significant weaknesses in some local church youth programs. The Lord has given me the opportunity over the last several years to visit a wide variety of churches. I have been in mega-churches and house churches, denominational churches and "non-denom" churches, conventional churches and innovative churches— and yes, I will admit that I have witnessed some youth ministries that I would characterize as "unsuccessful" because they are not truly fulfilling the Biblical mission of the church in the lives of their teenagers.

I have observed five distinct deficiencies and have attempted to describe them below.

Why Might High School Graduates Walk Away?

1. *Activity Based Ministry Philosophy*

    If the church's youth ministry is based upon programs and activities, graduates will most likely walk away after they graduate. Young adults can and will find their entertainment elsewhere. The appeal of amusement parks and hayrides fades away fairly quickly. In fact, many youth workers tell me that some of their high school juniors and seniors are actually dropping out of youth group for the same reasons.

    (Youth workers, please also be careful of running the same activity schedule year-after-year so that your seniors have the same basic schedule as ninth graders, or even seventh graders.

Believe me, they'll get bored and frustrated, and your youth program will grow old and tired as they mature through senior high school. I highly encourage you to build a growing level of accountability and ministry responsibilities into the structure of your youth ministry and raise the bar as your teenagers mature toward adulthood.)

2. *Program Based Ministry Philosophy*

Another reason why high school graduates walk away from regular involvement in church is if the youth group has been characterized by the rigid structure of a "boxed" youth program. There are youth ministry organizations out there that offer complete youth ministry programs and curriculum. Churches pay a fee or purchase the program, and the organization sends the church a complete youth ministry kit that is supposed to continue everything that church would need to run a successful youth program.

This approach is, in fact, designed to be terminal programs, with a specific, publicized ending point. There tends to be one final step or one top award to earn. That's the point. The students finish the program and they're done. What else is there to do? In the program-based approach to youth ministry it is very difficult to transfer the loyalty generated throughout the years of dedication to the program to the church as a whole. It's no wonder young people would walk away.

3. *Personality Based Ministry Philosophy*

A common characteristic of many church youth ministries is the tendency to center the ministry around the strong personality of a charismatic and magnetic youth pastor or youth leader. Strong personalities may attract impressionable high school students, and it seems to make sense for churches to do that, until the inevitable transition between personalities. If the teenagers are attracted to and ministered to by the presence of one strong personality it will be very difficult for them to transition into the adult ministries of the church without the involvement of that strong personality, or other equally strong personalities.

4. *Generationally Based Ministry Philosophy*

A church is making a mistake if it totally separates its youth from the overall life of the church. In the long run, this hurts students because they do not develop significant relationships with a number of influential adults.

I have spent a long time specializing in local church youth ministry and I am a strong proponent of peer ministry. Christian kids need friendships with other Christian kids. Plus, teenagers have always been better at reaching their peers than adult youth workers. However, a balanced youth ministry must feature strong inter-generational connections alongside traditional peer-to-peer youth groups. Dr. Chap Clark has stated that in order for graduating teens to stay in church following graduation, they will need positive relationships with five adults other than their parents.[2] I believe he's right. Involving young people in a broad community of believers that are committed to the growth and maturity of the next generation is critically important for their spiritual maturity and growth.

5. *Entertainment Based Ministry Philosophy*

> Akin to the "activity based" youth ministry is a narcissistic approach where churches seek to entertain teenagers by providing almost everything they want. If the kids want to go skiing, they go on ski trips. If the kids want to go swimming, they take them to the beach. This approach will ultimately produce self-absorbed and self-centered graduates who believe the church is all about them. When they are asked to transition into the church's adult ministries, they will struggle to fit into a program that is not centered around entertainment and narcissism. The undeveloped youth mindset may respond positively to this kind of approach, but adult maturity realizes there's more to life than getting everything I want.

We have all seen youth programs like the ones I have described above. The tendency is to look at these flaws and conclude that all youth ministry isn't working. Yet, it is imperative and essential to look at both sides of this issue.

CHAPTER 4

HOW CAN YOU MAKE YOUTH MINISTRY A PRIORITY IN YOUR CHURCH?

A FEW DAYS AFTER PRESENTING A youth ministry seminar I received a revealing phone call. The caller, a local church youth worker, made this evaluation of the church she attended: "The church leaders just don't see youth ministry as very important."

Perhaps every youth worker feels that way from time-to-time. We all wish the church had a greater vision for what youth ministry can do. However, I absolutely believe there are simple things every youth worker can do to help the entire church see the big picture of what a Biblical and effective youth ministry can bring to the overall church.

Here are five suggestions:

1. **Motivate older adults to pray for emerging generations – and start with the senior citizens!**

    One of the best ways to help your church develop a burden for youth is to encourage the older adults to pray intentionally and specifically for them by name. It's really very simple. Start by compiling a list of your church's teenagers. Then meet with your church's older adults. You could take a few moments and drop in on their Sunday School class. Ask them to pray for the teenagers by name. Remind them how important it is for them to pray for the church's youth. You could divide your list of names by each day of the week or assign specific students as prayer partners with specific adults.

I know of one youth pastor that made baseball card-sized cards for each student to encourage older adults to pray for the young people in their church. Another church regularly displayed photographs and names of students included in the church's digital announcements to remind the congregation to pray specifically for them.

The important thing is to do everything you can to motivate the adults to pray specifically for individual young people. Once they begin to pray regularly and intentionally for specific teenagers, the Lord will put a growing burden on their heart to help and encourage those students to live for God. You'll be amazed at how much this helps.

2. **Give your adults specific opportunities to see the younger generations actively living for the Lord.**

I am a big fan of connecting the generations in church. The Apostle Paul must have wanted that to happen, too. He wrote this in 1 Timothy 4:12: "Let no one despise your youth, but be an example to the believers…" Being an example requires exposure to others. Separating the generations does not give them any exposure to each other.

I am convinced that the older generations, in their hearts, want the same thing you do – for your church's young people to live for God! So, do whatever you can to give the older generations specific opportunities to see positive examples of your students living for the Lord and serving Him.

Perhaps the traditional "youth night" services (where the teenagers participate in every aspect of the service, such as announcements, worship, ushering, and preaching) are one way of doing that. But there are other tangible ways as well. Do anything you can do to give your teens specific and visible opportunities to serve the Lord in the church. For example, you could schedule work days for the students to invest in "sweat equity" in the church.

One youth pastor I know began teaching his church's senior citizens Sunday School class as a way to build positive relationships with that generation. On several occasions, he took them on a "field trip" to the youth class where they could see and hear the youth worship the Lord with fervency and enthusiasm. The seniors were also there to hear the announcements and the testimonies of the many, many ways the youth group served the Lord and actively witnessed for Him. The unity between those two generations in that church was absolutely contagious. It came because the teenagers in that youth group were a visible example to the older generations.

3. **Provide specific opportunities for the different generations to have interaction and fellowship with each other.**

Let's face it, most churches do not give the various generations even simple opportunities to get to know each other. Why not schedule and plan a simple fellowship time for your church's teenagers and older adults? Some churches ask their youth to put on a meal for the seniors. Other churches schedule a table-game night at the church. The actual ideas are almost endless. The important thing is for the youth and the older adults to get to know each other by encouraging them to tell their stories to the older generations. You'll be amazed at how positive this simple idea can be.

4. **Begin to provide ways for the different generations to pray with each other, but begin slowly.**

It may be threatening to schedule prayer times together as the first way to connect the generations. Serious prayer times should be intimate and can be intimidating if relationships are not built first. However, once the various generations have prayed for each other, and once they get to know each other–praying together can be a powerful connecting influence. You know how it is. People who pray *for* each other end up praying *with* each other. True inter-generational prayer services can be very positive for any church.

5. **Provide significant ways for younger people to serve alongside older people in established ministries.**

Encourage every adult in your church to recruit a younger person to serve alongside them in specific ministry responsibilities. This should be the expected norm in your church. If I had my way, I would make this an "executive order" and would require this idea to happen in every church. If someone leads a small group Bible study, they should be expected to find a younger person to serve as their assistant. Your sound room staff should be training younger people to someday replace them. Why not ask your church ushers to include young people on the team? And don't forget the worship team.

It would be a significant visual aid for the entire church to see older people and younger people serving the Lord together in your church's public music ministry. Church work days can be another opportunity for significant inter-generational relationships to develop. The important thing is to provide or create ways for the different generations to serve the Lord together.

I shared these five basic suggestions with the caller I referenced earlier, and I'm pleased to report amazing progress in that church. She has since let me know that their youth group was able to implement these ideas and the pastor, the other church leaders, and even the congregation were largely quite receptive to these ways of connecting the generations—which in turn helped that church see the youth workers' efforts with teenagers as important and even necessary.

I'm convinced these suggestions will work for you too!

CHAPTER 5

WHAT ARE SOME CHARACTERISTICS OF CHURCHES THAT HELP YOUNG PEOPLE GO ON FOR GOD?

So, WHAT TYPE OF YOUTH ministry helps its high school graduates transition into the overall life of the church, and what kind of church builds its various ministries harmoniously around a consistent philosophy? It is a powerful thing when the youth ministry, adult ministries, and parents and families are all on the same page. We must not forget that God instituted two distinct institutions—the family and the church.

I am absolutely convinced that a church's ministry philosophy must be consistently applied and implemented throughout the structure and programming for all age groups. Of course, your children's ministry will look differently than your ministry to teenagers and other generations. The various age groups have different needs, different methods of learning, and will be at varying levels of maturity. However, the philosophy and direction of ministry should be the same. The purpose or objective should be the same. All ministries must be focused on developing genuine and lasting spiritual maturity (Matthew 28:18-20, Ephesians 4:11-16, and 2

Timothy 3:10-17.) We are all trying to produce people who live for God and who go on growing in Him throughout their lives.

Here are five suggested ingredients that all churches should endeavor to include within the fabric of their total program for all age groups.

1. **Life-Related Bible Teaching**

   "...Be doers of the word, and not hearers only..." (James 1:22)

   Youth ministry has long led the way on incorporating the Bible into its structure. Youth ministry has taught us all about the importance of daily devotions, Scripture memory, and preaching via the ubiquitous "youth rally." But one of the most important aspects of youth ministry has been its emphasis on implementing Biblical truth into life. Most youth workers understand that the ultimate test of Bible teaching is not a one-hour lecture on Sunday mornings. It's living out your faith 24-7, all week long. That's something the entire church must learn – from the Sunday morning worship services to the adult Bible fellowship classes. High school students who have experienced the value of life-related Bible teaching while they were in high school would be much more likely to successfully transition into adult ministries if the church as a whole was set up to do that as well. This should be a clear mandate for all church leaders. Make sure the Bible is indeed taught this way throughout every ministry of their churches.

2. **Strong Inter-Generational Connections**

   "Having so fond an affection for you, we were well-pleased to impart to you not only the gospel of God but also our own lives, because you had become very dear to us."
   (1 Thessalonians 2:8)

It is imperative for churches to be intentional about developing positive, growing, and Godly inter-generational relationships. Older people need to see and sense the life, energy, and enthusiasm of youth; and younger generations need to learn from the wisdom, maturity, and life-experiences of older people. This mutual sharing and the life connections generated by it are what the church is all about. I really believe that high school graduates and young adults are much more likely to stay active in church if they have developed healthy and growing relationships with significant older adults. Young people are prone to walk away if their only true relationships in the church are with people their own age.

3. **Parental Consistency**

"For I am mindful of the sincere faith within you, which first dwelt in your grandmother Lois and your mother Eunice, and I am sure it is in you as well." (2 Timothy 1:5)

Remember high school algebra? If A = B and B = C, then A = C. In mathematics there are specific formulas with guaranteed, definite results. However, we all understand that the process of raising children does not come with pre-packaged, pre-arranged formulas. It's not that easy. In fact, parenting is one of the most difficult, yet most rewarding adventures in life. It is through parenting that one generation passes along the priorities of faith, belief, customs, traditions, and even life itself. Parents are the ones who normally develop the habit of church attendance and involvement into the lives of their family members. Parents are the ones who can make participation in church youth group a top priority – even higher in importance than schoolwork, activities, jobs, sports, or other involvements.

If church (and faithfully living for God for that matter) is a top priority for parents and if they are consistent in demonstrating that priority to their children, it is much more likely that the kids will grow up seeing church involvement as important for their lives as well. It's a manner of being genuine and being faithful over the long haul.

Churches and parents working in tandem will be a potent force in the lives of today's Christian young people. As I mentioned briefly above, God has developed two institutions – the family and the church. Wise parents and church leaders must work together with the common goal of seeing young people go on for God as they transition from infancy, through adolescence, and on into adulthood.

4. **Local Church Involvement**

"...held together by what every joint supplies, according to the proper working of each individual part..." (Ephesians 4:11-16)

It is important to remember that we are developing a ministry, not a program. Communities and man-made organizations can develop programs; but true ministry finds a foundation within the local church. It is imperative for "big church" and youth ministry to work together to make the church a place where everyone can be involved, not just attend. That's the picture found in passages like Ephesians 4:11-16. Therefore, getting students involved must be a significant ingredient of overall church life.

Wise youth workers must work alongside of Christian parents of teenagers to begin teaching and training young people to serve the Lord in and through the local church, to give financially to the church, and to actively participate in church-wide endeavors such as preaching, discipleship, fellowship, outreach, and worship. We must remember that we are involved in one church – not various age-group churches meeting separately in the same building.

5. **Welcoming & Accepting Community**

"But you must continue in the things which you have learned and been assured of, knowing from whom you have learned them, and that from childhood you have known the Holy Scriptures, which are able to make you wise for salvation through faith which is in Christ Jesus." (2 Timothy 3:14-15)

There's a final ingredient which also must be addressed, and that is the importance of making intentional and purposeful transitions between the various generational ministries of the church. Children, adolescents, and adults are uniquely different generations and therefore require distinctive peer-based approaches to ministry. I believe in the generational advantages of age-based children's ministry, youth ministry, and adult ministry. But let's face it, most churches are notoriously weak at helping people transition between the various ministry age groups. Youth workers should help pre-teens transition into youth ministry, and the church must help graduating high school seniors and maturing young adults transition into the adult ministries of the church. Too many times we kick graduating high schoolers out of youth group without helping them transition into the church's adult ministries. Churches should work hard to develop an accepting and welcoming environment in their adult ministries that actively encourages young people to participate in the life of the church.

Maybe I'm being somewhat idealistic here, but I believe this can happen. I believe that various church ministries must be on the same page, with the same objective—to see our maturing and growing young people grow up and go on for God! I really believe that if "big church" was organized purposefully to include the very best aspects of youth ministry and if churches developed a harmonious and unified philosophy of ministry throughout the various age groups, our young people would be much more likely to remain actively involved in church as teenagers and beyond their adolescent years long into adulthood.

CHAPTER 6

HOW CAN YOUR CHURCH DEVELOP AN INTER-GENERATIONAL APPROACH TO YOUTH MINISTRY?

W<small>E HAVE ALL HEARD ABOUT</small> an "oxymoron", right? It's a figure of speech where seemingly contradictory terms appear together. Here are some illustrations:

- Accurate estimate
- Act naturally
- Adult children
- Casual dress
- Sanitary landfill
- Airline food[1]

Here is another apparent oxymoron that may have some validity to it: inter-generational youth ministry. I wholeheartedly believe in the importance of connecting the various generations in the church, but also to balance that approach alongside a vibrant youth ministry. There's no conflict here. I believe in youth ministry, and I have been actively involved in it in some form or another for more than 45 years. But I have a growing conviction that if churches totally separate their teenagers from the overall life of the church, they are making a big mistake.

Older adults need the life and energy of youth – and young people need the wisdom and maturity of older adults. The church was designed by God to be inter-generational, and the generations need each other. I am convinced that today's churches can and should balance their programming and methods so that peer ministry can exist and thrive alongside of inter-generational ministry.

Our students need Godly adults to be actively involved in their lives. It is essential for the spiritual development of youth that older, Godly adults take the initiative to build growing relationships with them.

Here are some suggestions on how to implement an inter-generational youth ministry:

1. **Recruit a team of Godly, caring adults to serve as lay youth workers in your church.**

   With or without a paid youth pastor, your church needs a team of spiritually mature and caring adults to work with teenagers. Please notice the plurality of my terms. Team ministry, with different models of adults who can reach and minister different teens, is so important. The main responsibility of any lay youth worker must be to build relationships with teens. That's the key. Opportunities to teach and disciple will grow out of positive relationships.

   Small group leaders are another level of adult interaction with students. Be sure to find adults who can guide discussions around the Scriptures and who can think on their feet in case the teens ask difficult questions. I think it's also wise to look for small group leaders who are able and willing to interact with the students on occasions outside of the small group. (Some churches are organizing their entire small group ministry around inter-generational connections; and of course, this would add an interesting dynamic to this type of ministry structure.)

2. **Utilize church leaders, parents of teenagers, and other significant adults to serve in your youth group.**

Another way to build adults into the lives of the young people in your church is to use significant adults in various ways within the fabric of your existing youth ministry. Here are some practical ideas to consider:

- Ask some parents of teenagers or other adults to accompany your group on youth events or trips, almost in the role of a chaperone.
- Ask top-level church leaders to speak, teach, or otherwise participate in youth group meetings.
- Ask the lead pastor or other pastoral staff members to teach on a specific topic in youth group.
- Ask mature adults who have unique life experiences to minister to students who are facing some of the same experiences.
- Give older, Godly adults the opportunity to share their story (or their testimony) with teenagers.

(Of course, you'll need to be cognizant of your church's policy on child protection clearances and use of background checks before making these decisions.)

3. **Ask Godly parents of teenagers to build healthy, growing relationships with their kids' friends.**

Parents of kids in your church can be the ideal people to minister to their kids' friends – especially if you have young people involved in your ministry who are from dysfunctional or hurting home situations. When our own children were teenagers, we often encouraged them to invite their friends over to our house. This provided a safe atmosphere for our kids and gave us the opportunity to get to know their friends. It might be a good idea to be intentional about making this kind of thing happen with some of the parents of teens in your church.

4. **Motivate your church's senior citizens to pray specifically and intentionally for young people–by name.**

I am excited about a growing trend around the country to intentionally involve senior citizens in specific ways with teenagers and young adults. This absolutely must start with prayer. Do whatever you can to motivate your church's oldest adults to pray specifically, by name for the young people. This simple practice will put a growing burden on their hearts for the students. Honestly, it has the potential to revolutionize your church and shatter the generation gap!

5. **Select certain older adults to mentor the young people in church, especially those who are serving in specific avenues of ministry.**

Mentoring is another way to specifically connect the generations in the church. That's the idea found in Titus 2:1-8, where the

Apostle Paul instructed Titus to encourage older people to mentor younger people in that first century church.

Church-based mentoring begins in the church foyer when older adults take the initiative to greet, and then build growing relationships with younger people. The best mentors tend to have something specific in common with the individuals they are mentoring. This might include an interest in a skill or craft, a vocational similarity, a geographical connection, or comparable life experiences.

I am convinced that by implementing some of the ideas listed above your church can develop a truly inter-generational youth ministry. It is not an oxymoron!

CHAPTER 7

HOW CAN ALL GENERATIONS BE A PART OF THE CHURCH?

TAKING A WALK THROUGH MOST traditional churches on a Sunday morning reveals a trend in church programming.

The children gather with their Sunday School teachers in the church's basement. A group of teenagers meet with a couple of young-looking adult leaders in an upstairs loft. Most of the adults are scattered throughout the auditorium, while a cluster of senior citizens assemble in the church office. Other than the involvement of a few loyal workers and helpers, the various generations have almost nothing to do with each other during a typical church's Sunday schedule.

A Brief History of Segregating the Generations in the Church

Where did the idea come from that it is a good thing to separate the generations? The conventional church structure, where the various generations are almost totally disconnected from each other, is a fairly recent trend that has been adapted from a variety of religious and cultural customs.

One of the originators of age-segregated programming was the wide acceptance of the Sunday School as an essential ingredient of church educational endeavors. According to church historians, "The Sunday School movement began in Britain in the 1780's. The Industrial Revolution had resulted in many children spending all week long working in factories... Saturday was part of the regular work week. Sunday, therefore, was the only available time for these children to gain some education. The English Anglican evangelical Robert Raikes (1725-1811) was the key promoter of the movement. It soon spread to America as well. Denominations and non-denominational organizations caught the vision and energetically began to create Sunday Schools. Within decades, the movement had become extremely popular. By the mid-19th century, Sunday School attendance was a near universal aspect of childhood."[1]

Ancient Jewish culture included a "coming of age" custom that is pictured in Scripture when Jesus' human parents took Him to the Temple in Jerusalem as a 12-year-old. (The narrative is found in Luke 2:41-52, and the Jewish regulation is explained in Deuteronomy 16:16.) The historical disconnect between generations was well-defined by this "rite of passage" as described concerning Christ Himself. Children learned at one level of education; adults were taught at another.

This nation's compulsory education system also fostered the idea of age-based segregation. Earlier educational methodologies were centered around a strong parental influence over their children. Parents, often especially fathers, were actively involved in their children's education and vocational training. This hands-on connection with close adults provided tangible inter-generational relationships between children and adults. Once children were separated from their parents for several hours each day, their closest interpersonal relationships became with their peers, who vastly outnumbered their teachers.

Rationale for Age-Specific Ministry

Over the years, the church accepted and implemented that age-specific educational approach. Sunday Schools, youth groups, and children's clubs became a common practice that divided the generations for age-specific programming. Adult educational ministries followed, and the traditional church rapidly became disconnected generationally.

Obviously, there are positive reasons for separating into age group categories for local church ministry. The division into age groups allows maturing young people to learn at their own level (1 Corinthians 13:11, 1 Timothy 5:1-2, and 1 John 12-14). It provides important fellowship and community with peers (Hebrews 10:25 and Acts 2:42), and evangelistic opportunities often happen best with people at the same stage of life (Acts 17:16-34 and 18:1-4).

Rationale for Inter-Generational Connections

However, there are also very valid reasons for building growing and positive inter-generational relationships in the church. The most obvious reasons are that young people can learn much from the life experience and Godly faithfulness of older adults (see Titus 2:1-8), and older people can also learn from the example and zeal of young people (see 1 Timothy 4:12). The Scriptures are emphatic that the various generations need each other (Psalm 78:1-8 and Psalm 71:18).

Christ Himself modeled the importance of building of inter-generational relationships in the ministry He had with His twelve disciples, most of whom were younger people at the time. The Apostle Paul also demonstrated the significance of inter-generational connections – for example with his ministry with young men like John Mark (Acts 12 and 13:1-5) and Timothy (Acts 16:1-5).

A Brief Description of Different Generational Ministries

There are three basic approaches to the way most churches program their services, activities, and functions. The first would be a "one-generational" structure, where the various age groups almost exclusively gather in generational groupings. For example (like what was illustrated above), the children meet in one location, the teenagers in another, and the adults meet somewhere else.

The next approach would be "multi-generational" scheduling where the various generations would gather alongside each other, maybe even in the same room, but who have very little, if any, connections with each other.

The last generational style of ministry programming is when a church provides specific occasions for the various generations to connect with each other using "inter-generational" methods and practices. This is when older people actively seek out younger people to encourage them and mentor them in a way that helps emerging generations to grow up to go on for God, and when younger people look to older people as examples and models of faithfully living for God.

Building Inter-Generational Relationships

A balance of programming between the three styles of ministry is probably the key to a healthy church. At present, it seems as if many churches are out of balance on the side of age-segregated ministries. Perhaps it is time to work on techniques that churches can use to help develop inter-generational connections.

Here are some practical ways everyone can build growing inter-generational relationships in the church.

1. *Pray specifically and individually for members of other generations.*

   This practice should begin with the older generations in the church who can set the example for helping to connect the age groups through prayer. The older generations in the church should commit to make a habit of praying by name for members of emerging generations in the church. Praying specifically in this manner will help develop an increasing burden in hearts for those they are praying for, and there will be less cross-generational tension in the church because of this intentional prayer.

2. *Serve the Lord together with people from other generations.*

   Each ministry position and opportunity in the church should include a mentoring component that allows for older people to serve alongside younger people. This inter-generational idea should be an integral aspect of serving the Lord in and through the local church. For example, older teachers could mentor younger teachers, experienced ushers and greeters could be examples for less experienced ones, and even elders and pastors should be motivated to share their expertise and knowledge with younger leaders. Of course, churches must adhere to strict child protection policies and obtain the proper background checks and clearances.

3. *Schedule times of fellowship and personal interaction between the generations.*

Specific time slots should be set aside for the different generations to have time for fellowship with each other. This is most likely not to happen unless the church is intentional about scheduling opportunities. Some churches utilize their youth groups to prepare a meal or other activity for the older adults. Other churches just schedule fellowship times (like "board game nights") to allow time for older members to connect and build relationships with younger people – including time for them to share their stories of God's faithfulness to them over the course of their lives.

Maybe it's time for another fictional tour around the traditional church buildings – this time with a vision for balanced church ministries that connect the generations building positive and growing relationships with each other. Churches do not need to totally segregate the generations but should seek to organize church functions that are generationally balanced. Growing and healthy relationships can be developed between the generations with initiative and intentionality.

This article first appeared: https://www.christianity.com/wiki/church/how-all-ages-can-be-a-part-of-the-church.html.

CHAPTER 8

HOW CAN YOUTH MINISTRY IMPACT "BIG CHURCH"?

THE APOSTLE PAUL HAD IT right when he challenged his student, Timothy, to "let no one despise your youth, but be an example to the believers in word, in conduct, in love, in spirit, in faith, in purity" (1 Timothy 4:12).

The context of this verse gives clear indication that this great missionary leader was encouraging young Timothy to make sure that his private life substantiated his public message. In other words, he was telling us that young people can and should be examples to older people. From reading this passage, one can conclude that others in the Ephesus church were older (maybe significantly so) than Timothy. Yet, he was instructed to be an example to them. This same principle can be a clear mandate for teenagers today.

Our students can have a church-wide impact. I've seen it happen and probably so have you. Students come back from a conference, camp, or mission trip fired up to do something great for God. The Lord has been at work in their hearts, and they come home totally on fire and completely dedicated to the cause of Christ. The adults hear their testimonies and sense their passion to do something great for God.

This genuine enthusiasm is contagious and infectious to people of all generations.

I've seen this phenomenon lead to a spirit of true revival that has effectively spread throughout the entire church. Let me tell you quickly about one such occasion in a church I know. It started when the Lord used one of the volunteer youth workers to lead a teenage girl to Christ. This 16-year-old new believer then led her best friend to Christ. These two baby Christians quickly became motivated to start a Bible study to reach other friends for Christ in their local public school. Almost at the same time, some of our regular attendees had recently returned from a major youth conference and were eager to see God continue to use that event to change lives back home. One young man prayed to accept Christ and another made a public decision to be more vocal about his faith. On one particular Sunday almost twenty teenagers made public decisions to commit their lives to Christ. Soon several of their parents followed them, and then other adults. Without any exaggeration, this sense of revival very quickly spread throughout the entire church. God used two new Christians and a handful of other students returning from a youth conference to impact that whole church body.

I don't want to presume that I can identify here in this short article all the factors that the Lord can use to bring this kind of church-wide revival, but I do believe Paul's instruction to young Timothy that he could be an example to other believers.

I find it interesting that 2 Timothy 4:12 identifies some specific areas in which young people can be an example to older Christians. ("...in word, in conduct, in love, in spirit, in faith, in purity.") Students can indeed impact others through their words, their manner of life, their love, their enthusiasm, their dedication to God, and through their moral purity.

The key is that the youth ministry should have personal, public, and positive exposure to other ages within the church. Let me explain.

1. **Make sure that your students have personal exposure to other age groups in your church.**

   Students need to get to know the adults, and the adults need to get to know the students. It's that simple. We must build significant interpersonal and inter-generational relationships in our churches. I believe that this process starts when godly adults are willing to take the initiative to develop these nurturing and mutually beneficial relationships with kids. Don't expect most kids to go out of their way to get to know adults. That's probably not going to happen. (Just make sure that your church's child protection policies are known and enforced.)

   The adults in your church will probably need to be taught to be proactive and seek out individual students to mentor. It's a well-reported fact that most of today's teenagers are interested in positive and growing relationships with adults. But remember that the obligation is on the adults to make these relationships happen.

   This exposure can happen in several very effective ways. I am a firm believer in making sure your students are welcome to actively participate in all areas of your church ministry. Also, youth workers need to plan creative and well-organized events for the adults and teenagers to interact together. You will undoubtedly find that you need to motivate both adults and teenagers to be involved; but once you hold these positive events on a regular basis, the existing walls of aloofness and intimidation will break down.

I encourage all youth workers to brainstorm and then implement other ways to help the different generations in your church develop intentional and growing interpersonal relationships between members of the various generations.

2. **Give your students public exposure to other age groups in your church.**

It is also important to give students *public* exposure to your church. I admit that I am a long-time fan of "youth services" and other ways for the teens to interact with other generations in a public way. The first time I ever preached was during a youth night service where the teenagers took over our church's entire evening service. But please recognize that I do not believe that these periodic services should be the only way for teenagers to get involved in your church. If these youth services are the only public exposure the students have, it can lead to the feeling that the teenagers are actually "on show" every so often and not really a vital part of the church.

Why not let your teenagers take an active role in the regular ministries of your church? I think that some talented teenagers should participate in the worship team during regularly scheduled church services for example. I like to encourage and train other teenagers to serve as ushers or greeters. I also think students should be encouraged and taught to tithe and to participate in church business meetings. After all, this is their church too. They should be involved.

Young people should also be given the opportunity to serve with adults in your church's kid's ministry, or other key areas of service. The key here is the part about serving alongside adults. This team ministry can be an amazingly effective way of training future leaders and servants for ongoing church involvement. When adults and teenagers work alongside each other, they see each other's heart for God and for other people. This, too, will break down the walls of suspicion and negativity between the generations.

3. **Give godly students positive exposure to other age groups.**

Another thought that I want to emphasize concerning exposing teenagers to the other generations in church is that the exposure should be *positive* exposure. You want the adults to see kids who love the Lord and are passionate about serving Him. It is contagious to see godly kids who are genuinely enthusiastic about the Lord. That cannot be ignored! Therefore, make sure you give this exposure to students who are not "carnal" (1 Corinthians 3:1-3) or living in sin. I am not saying that external things are the most important characteristic. Please do not hold your teenagers to higher external standards than you require of the adults who serve. But I am saying that the students who participate in other organized church ministries should be living for the Lord. (I also believe that this standard should be expected of adults, by the way.)

God's Word is very clear on this idea, "He who is faithful in what is least is faithful also in much; and he who is unjust in what is least is unjust also in much" (Luke 16:10). However, unless there are habits of unconfessed, public sin, all Christians should be actively involved in church ministry (Ephesians 4:11–16).

What a powerful visual aid to see students who love the Lord and want to serve Him! Adults can't resist the excitement and eagerness from teenagers who are truly motivated about living for the Lord. In fact, when adults see the passion and enthusiasm of teenagers who really want to live for God, the external things will become almost non-issues.

I also want to emphasize that the ministry experience should be positive. In other words, you want students to enjoy serving the Lord and to do so without being coerced or made to feel guilty for not serving. Ministry should be fun and rewarding. It is a blast to serve the Lord. Yes, it is difficult at times, but look at all the Lord did for us. We should want to serve Him and live for Him because of our desire to be obedient to Him. That's what we want from our students as well.

Yes, I believe that Paul had it right. Students can be an example to "big church"!

SECTION 2

Reaching and Ministering to Emerging Generations

CHAPTER 9

HOW CAN WE REACH EMERGING GENERATIONS WITH THE GOSPEL?

Missionaries, church leaders, and youth workers have long understood the importance of evangelism to the world's unreached people groups. According to one source, an "unreached people group" is a cohort of people that lacks enough followers of Christ and resources to evangelize their own without some outside assistance.[1]

The history of missions is lined with the stories of how God placed a growing burden on the hearts of motivated individuals and their sending churches to reach out around the globe to lost people. Because of the enduring influence of the Gospel, the church is thriving in places that are currently closed to outside missionary assistance; for example, parts of China and Korea. Since the inception of His church, God has used a variety of called and visionary evangelists to make an enduring impact for Christ.

The history of youth ministry also reflects the visionary leadership of highly motivated people who observed the spiritual and cultural needs of younger generations and who believed that God was directing them to do something to reach young people with the Gospel. Contemporary youth ministry actually started out of a burden to see young people come to Christ.

Yet, unreached people groups remain - with apologies to missionary purists for using that broad definition of this term. The United States is currently experiencing the growing influence of emerging generations. "Generation Z" (or Gen Z),[2] this country's least-Christian "unreached people group" ever will be followed closely by members of "Generation Alpha",[3] currently the world's youngest generation.

These new generations are digital natives,[4] the majority of whom are from dysfunctional and non-traditional households;[5] plus, they have come-of-age in a post-Christian[6] and post-church[7] culture.

Gen Z is the generation currently in high school or just starting college – and is over 74 million people in size.[8] Using the above listed definition and classifications as our guide, this positions them as one of the largest unreached people groups in the world. Their generational standing as emerging adults also makes them a strategic target for ministry endeavors and evangelistic efforts of the church.

Generation Alpha, born approximately 2010 to 2025 and probably a much smaller generation[9] than the previous two cohorts based on current birth rates,[10] will be comprised of approximately 52 million people in the United States. This is the generation that will be most affected by the lasting ramifications of the Covid virus and will probably face continuing struggles with the negative emotions of fear and uncertainty.

Like Gen Z, Alpha's will grow up in a post-Christian and post-church world and, as the offspring of Millennial generation parents,[11] are not likely to see church or religious organizations as an important priority in their own lives and schedules. Some sociologists are also observing that members of this generation will also face a "post-family" culture[12] as well, where the perceived American ideal of a family unit will not be the norm.

There is also growing indication that churches will need to retool and revamp their children's and youth ministries to reach them with the Gospel and to continue to have effective ministries to these emerging generations.

More than ever, church leaders and youth workers in this country will need to think and act more like cross-cultural missionaries to reach these new generations. Here are a few basic missional suggestions to consider when thinking about how to reach out to today's two youngest generations.

1. **Go to them, instead of asking them to come to church functions.**

   The Great Commission begins with an assumption that believers would "go" with the Gospel (Matthew 28:19-20). The early church's great missionary endeavors, led by Barnabas and Saul (soon to be called the Apostle Paul), also began with a commitment to "go" (Acts 13:1-5). *Going* has been the central passion of missions ever since – and that's what it will take to impact this people group as well.

   Today's youngest generations are burdened with busy schedules and conflicting priorities. They are more inclined to participate in weekend sports than they are to attend church services. Youth workers should not complain about how today's teenagers are unfaithful to the church's scheduled youth meetings, but instead must commit to find ways to reach out to them through their overly-scheduled school, work, and extracurricular activities. To reach this generation, youth workers will need to go outside the walls of church buildings to develop growing relationships with young people and their parents.

2. **Find creative ways to share the Gospel and to teach Biblical truth, instead of looking for ways to entertain them.**

It's not a pun or a play on words, the mission of missions was and is to share the Gospel. That must be the focus of today's ministry to younger generations as well. The lasting legacy of the history of both missions and youth ministry are the stories of how God used visionary leaders to use their creative energy to reach the next generation for Christ. They looked at culture as an opportunity, not an obstacle, to impact others with the Gospel. They weren't overly concerned about ways to attract people to their programs. They were highly motivated to find ways to teach God's Word creatively and effectively to others.

Reaching Gen Z and Alpha will demand an entrepreneurial spirit where today's visionary leaders develop culturally relevant ways to communicate God's truth to new generations.

3. **Adapt strategies for cultural impact, instead of accepting traditional norms of ministry.**

Cross-cultural missionaries understand that it's probably not productive to utilize American or western methodologies to reach people from other social or ethnic perspectives and backgrounds. Outreach and ministry strategies must be adapted for the cultural mores of the targeted people group.

Church ministry did not look the same in Antioch as it did in the Jerusalem church in Acts. These seven churches in Revelation each had unique strengths and weaknesses that were sometimes born out of various cultural backgrounds. For example, the Apostle John's rebuke to the Laodiceans in Revelation 3:14-16 about being "lukewarm" was because of their city's vast use of a distribution of water.[13] "Cold" was refreshing and invigorating, while "hot" was soothing and even fervent. That ancient city's water supply offered both extremes to the residents. However, "lukewarm" was considered to be tepid and unappealing. Their geography helped them visualize and understand the truth being taught. Likewise, cultural and geographical differences today provide unique challenges and opportunities for the contemporary church as well.

4. **Expect opposition, instead of believing that most people will want to hear what we say.**

The earliest missionaries faced serious opposition and oppression. They were confronted by false teachers, they experienced physical torment and harassment, some were beaten, jailed, and ultimately even martyred for their desire to spread the message of Jesus Christ. It is not a stretch to think that the church may be headed toward another time when those in Christ's service can expect persecution.

Generation Z and Generation Alpha have grown up with a post-modern, pluralistic mindset. Researchers report that the leading religious influence of today's American culture is "moralistic, therapeutic deism",[14] a school of thought that honors and promotes the well-being of "self" and a person's own goals as the highest cause in life. No longer do most American young people see Christianity as a viable option for them personally.[15] It is now imperative for American churches to look at their outreach endeavors to emerging generations with the reality of facing opposition.

5. **Prioritize and utilize team ministry, instead of thinking that ministry is for individuals.**

Today's missionaries and youth workers must realize the days of the "lone ranger" are long gone. There may have been a time in the history of missions where one individual sensed the call of God and headed out all alone to the place where God was leading them. However, from the account of the first mission trip ever in Acts 13, until today's current 21st century approaches, God tends to use teams that are highly-committed and complimentarily-gifted to accomplish His work.

The same is true in youth ministry. An example of this can be found in the story of John Mark in the New Testament. He grew up in a Christian home as a church kid, and then was mentored by Barnabas, Paul, and Peter. A variety of Godly adults were used to help him grow from a kid with potential, through times of ministry failure, to someone that God used in significant ways for eternity. Churches today must likewise build teams of Godly older adults who can and will have a significant impact on members of this generation who crave and desperately need caring adults in their lives.

The United States is on the verge of a huge cultural shift as members of emerging generations mature and take on a growing level of influence on society. They will not have the same generational perspectives of the Millennials or Gen X'ers who came before them. They will indeed be a large and quite "unreached" people group with incredible spiritual and social issues facing them. Churches that want effective and successful ministries to children and teenagers will need to take a missionary approach to reaching them for Jesus Christ. Those who do will have a lasting impact for eternity.

CHAPTER 10

WHAT SHOULD EVERY YOUTH WORKER LEARN ABOUT GENERATION Z?

THERE MAY BE A MINISTRY "seismic shift" headed toward the American church!

A seismic shift can be defined as sudden or dramatic change that happens in a very short period of time.

Pastors and other church leaders need to realize that due to the cultural influence of Generation Z, the church may be facing an unprecedented change in the way that a majority of people in this country look at church programming. Often referred to as "Gen Z", this generation is composed of today's college-age young adults and current senior high young people. Although some researchers use other time periods, most identify Gen Z as being born between 1995 and 2010.[1]

Gen Z is a cohort of approximately 65 million people,[2] and will ultimately comprise about 40% of the entire US population.[3]

As researchers and social scientists are reporting, this generation is already incredibly influential, and they are about to make a massive and long-lasting change on every institution they touch–including the church. As one respected youth worker puts it, it's time to stop "doing Millennial ministry"[4] and recognize that a new generation has arrived. The church and church leaders must adapt accordingly.

It's important for pastors to understand that members of Gen Z have come of age in a culture of significant religious and cultural influences. These influences include the mass departure from the church by young adults (see *You Lost Me: Why Young Christians are Leaving the Church and Rethinking Faith*), a dwindling loyalty toward denominational or institutional affiliations (see *Rise of the Nones: Understanding and Reaching the Religiously Unaffiliated*, by James Emery White), a move toward a post-Christian and post-church mentality (see *Youth Ministry in a Post-Christian World: A Hopeful Wake-Up Call*, by Brock Morgan), and a growing number of non-traditional, broken, or dysfunctional households (see *Households of Faith*, published by Barna Group).

Here are five practical insights for pastors and other church leaders to consider as they develop creative and functional ministries to reach and minister to members of Gen Z.

1. **They crave the communication of truth in an environment where they can ask difficult and serious questions.**

   This is not a generation that will be attracted by entertainment or fluff. They are seeking truth and will respond positively to the clear exposition of Scripture and confident presentations of the Gospel. They are seeking real answers to their most difficult questions. A recent study from Barna Research tells readers to create the space for them to "feel the freedom to ask the big questions".[5] This begins by making church services and Bible studies places they feel are welcoming and non-threatening.

This is truly a post-Christian generation. One author puts it this way, "Perhaps the most defining mark of members of Generation Z… is their spiritual illiteracy… They do not know what the Bible says. They do not know the basics of Christian belief or theology."[6] To reach members of Generation Z, pastors must see that church is more than a once-a-week lecture and worship time. Church programming will need to feature ways to creatively teach Gen Z solid doctrinal truth with methods that provide opportunities to them to apply that truth to their everyday lives.

2. **They are looking to develop strong relationships in a culture of increasingly dysfunctional and broken households.**

Gen Z'ers are more likely than other recent generations to grow up in broken, unstable, or dysfunctional homes. One researcher put it this way, "Churches that want to understand and serve teens and young adults should focus first on true household ministry, and not just family ministry".[7] This means that more and more living situations in this culture will be comprised of "households" instead of traditional family units. According to one author, members of Generation Z are growing up with in an increasing number of single-parent homes; a growing number of cohabiting, non-married parents; a rising number of homes with single mothers; and an increasing number of same-sex couples.[8] These statistics should motivate pastors to lead their churches to be a "family" for those in today's culture from non-traditional and fractured households.

3. **Christian members of Gen Z are looking for ways to share their faith and want to learn how to witness effectively.**

Probably somewhat contrary to popular beliefs, about 75% of this generation who claim to be Christians and living for God report that they feel responsible to tell others about their faith.[9] This is a generation that feels very strongly about living on mission. They want to be involved in something that matters for eternity. Churches should capitalize on this renewed emphasis on evangelism by developing creative avenues for them to present the Gospel and share their faith with others.

This generation also feels a heightened sense of responsibility and stewardship. For example, they won't understand why most church buildings in this country remain unused throughout the week. Long gone are the days of church buildings that feature a large number of small meeting rooms that were once used for a wide variety of age-group programming. This won't make sense to Gen Z'ers. They'll want to figure out ways for churches to use their buildings for outreach functions to the community.

Since this is the most multi-ethnic generation in history, they will also be very open to share the Gospel cross-culturally. The world feels quite small to this generation and many of them will be excited about the potential of short-term mission trips, either internationally or to cross-cultural areas within the United States.

4. **Churches must utilize technology to communicate to this generation in a culture that is progressively disloyal and over-scheduled.**

Members of Generation Z are truly digital natives. They've had internet-connected devices in their pockets since they were young children. They likely grew up in homes that allowed them almost ubiquitous access to various digital smartphones and tablets; and they attended schools where teachers gave them internet-based assignments on their own iPads, or Chromebooks since kindergarten or pre-school. They are more comfortable with their digital Bibles than printed copies, and probably use their phones for daily devotions and in-depth Bible study. They also are very likely to fact-check what preachers or Bible teachers say, instead of just accepting what they hear as truth.

Technology is a game-changer for the American church. This doesn't mean that Gen Z will reject low-tech methods of communication. In fact, old-fashioned, lecture-style preaching may seem refreshing and genuine to them. Pastors should remember that this generation does not need the church to try to impress them with the church's technological prowess. They're quite capable of creating or locating their own quality digital content. However, due to this generation's busy schedules, it will be important for churches to utilize various means of technology to make sermons, seminars, publications, and other materials available for them to find on their own schedules on the church's website.

Today's pastors have undoubtedly noticed that "practicing Christians" are only attending church approximately one Sunday each month.[10] This trend is very likely to continue with members of Generation Z. Their lives will tend to be quite over-scheduled, with other personal priorities being more important to them than regular church attendance and involvement. Plus, Gen Z does not possess an innate loyalty to any denomination, church, or church function.[11] This practice will necessitate that pastors employ the use of modern technology to communicate regularly and successfully to them.

5. **Churches should be intentional about developing growing inter-generational relationships and connections.**

This generation is being forged by two seemingly conflicting pressures. As mentioned earlier, they are more likely to grow up in households without consistent parental influences, and they appreciate the influence of significant older adults. Their lives have been lined by a litany of coaches, teachers, youth workers, small group leaders, and other caring adults. Of course, churches must develop and institute carefully crafted child protection policies that safeguard kids from sinful adult predators. When these policies are followed, today's teenagers and young adults will profit greatly from the influence of Godly older adult mentors.

The practice of segregating and isolating young people from other generations has helped fuel their departure from the church following their years in high school. Emerging adults are not likely to commit to a church's adult ministries unless they have formed growing relationships with a variety of Godly adults in the church prior to their graduation from high school. Churches will need to restructure their programming efforts to balance peer ministries with growing inter-generational connections for Gen Z.

The American church is indeed facing a seismic shift as members of Generation Z move through adolescence into adulthood. "Business as usual" will not work. Pastors will need to retool and rethink their approach to ministry programming to be effective with today's emerging adults. Gen Z is here!

This article originally appeared: https://www.crosswalk.com/church/pastors-or-leadership/urgent-insights-on-gen-z-that-every-pastor-needs-to-know.html.

CHAPTER 11

WHY SHOULD YOUTH WORKERS LEARN NOW ABOUT GENERATION ALPHA?

TIME FLIES – THAT'S FOR sure!

It seemed like we were just talking about the Millennial Generation and their mark on culture when Generation Z came along. Millennials were the ones who were going to change everything – especially the way we did ministry. But then we were told to adjust our strategies because the new generation, Gen Z, would see life differently, and it would take new methodologies to reach them.

Of course, there is something particularly important about staying culturally relevant. Youth workers, maybe more than other ministry leaders, must understand the cultural influences that our students are experiencing while staying true to the teaching and practice of Biblical principles.

Our youth ministry forefathers led the way for us. Robert Raikes, the founder of the Sunday School movement in the 1700s, looked at what was happening in society and launched a ministry to reach kids by teaching them the Bible. Visionary leaders like Jack Wyrtzen and Percy Crawford in New York City and Torrey Johnson in Chicago rented stadiums to host youth rallies in the 1940s to reach an emerging youth culture with the Gospel. About the same time, para-church organizations like *Young Life* and *Youth for Christ* began to connect with kids in America's communities and public schools.

Christian colleges offered youth ministry majors and churches hired vocational youth pastors. Curriculum publishers produced youth materials and books, and youth ministry organizations like *Youth Specialties* became a part of a new youth ministry movement with the grand purpose to reach a new generation.[1]

But times changed and teenagers changed. Baby Boomers were replaced by the members of Generation X, who were followed by the Millennials and then Generation Z. Now it's time for youth workers to realize that a new generation of young people is on the cultural horizon.

The leading edge of "Generation Alpha" (their name coined by Australian researcher, Mark McCrindle[2]) is currently in upper elementary. They are the age group born between 2010–2025, and will be the first generation to be born entirely in the 21st Century. Alphas are likely to be the generation most affected by COVID-19 and are growing up in a world quite different from any other previous generation.

Today's youth workers are facing a new opportunity to develop culturally relevant and Biblically-based ministries for a new generation of students. Soon, the first wave of Generation Alpha will be teenagers. In ten years, they will be young adults and the latest generation that everyone is talking about. It is imperative that youth workers understand that they need to learn all they can to prepare to minister to our newest generation.

Why Learn About Generation Alpha Now?

Here are five reasons why youth workers must make it a priority to learn about Alphas now:

1. *Today's children will grow up.*

   This sounds too obvious, but it's true. One of the most important reasons to connect with pre-teens is because it is easier to reach them while they are young. If we do not build positive relationships with them now, there is a real likelihood that they will grow up without an important Godly influence on their lives.

2. *Many kids make lasting spiritual decisions when they are young.*

   It has been true for several generations. Most people make spiritual decisions while they are young. One researcher says that nine out of ten Christians accept Jesus before the age of 18.[3] Church leaders would be advised to develop intentional and culturally relevant ways to creatively share the Gospel with today's kids.

3. *Generation Alpha is part of your congregation now.*

   Too often, youth leaders ignore their church's ministry to children until they get to be teenagers. Of course, many youth workers are busy and don't need anything else on their plates. But strategically, it is important to understand that today's youngest generation is already a key target group for your youth ministry in the near future.

4. *Reaching kids helps churches connect with today's households.*

Today's children are growing up in a rapidly changing culture. Demographics reveal a growing number of non-traditional and dysfunctional households.[4] Taking the initiative to share the Gospel with kids might give churches the opportunity to connect with those households in our communities.

5. *Children are trend-setters and are great predictors of the future.*

Maybe the most important reason for today's youth workers to learn all they can about Generation Alpha is that kids are trend-setters with the ability to influence the future. Advertisers understand this and are targeting children now with a wide range of products and services. Real leaders understand the importance of being able to anticipate upcoming trends and develop ways to connect with people as time progresses.

Before we know it, a new generation will be a part of our ministries. Like other age groups, Generation Alpha has the potential to make a significant change in culture and in our churches.

CHAPTER 12

HOW CAN YOU HELP TEENAGERS DEVELOP A LOYALTY TO THEIR CHURCH?

ARE YOUR TEENAGERS MORE LOYAL to your youth ministry than they are to the church as a whole?

I'm wondering if that may be part of the reason why so many young adults are leaving the church after they graduate from high school. Maybe it's because we have unintentionally isolated teenagers from the overall life of the church so much that they don't actually see it as *their* church. They may love our youth ministries, but they often don't see the connection to "big church."

Youth workers must remember that youth ministry was never designed as a terminal program – with a specific ending point for the students to finish and then walk away. Our goal must be their long-term spiritual maturity. As youth workers, we want young people to come to Christ, grow closer to Him as they mature, and to serve Him for the rest of their lives as active members of His church.

Here are five things that any church can do to help youth build loyalty to the church:

1. **Teach them the importance of God's church.**

   Loyalty begins with an understanding of what God's church is all about. Perhaps you can develop a series of lessons on the church. Or you could take them through Acts, the Epistles, and even the 7 churches in Revelation to give them exposure to what the Bible says about the church. Teach them basic ecclesiology, and your church polity. There are lots of materials out there to help you with this, but if you feel uncomfortable doing this series yourself, I'm sure your lead pastor could offer some suggestions or resource materials to help you.

2. **Provide opportunities for them to serve in the church.**

   Loyalty also comes through what some would call "sweat equity". Give your students practical opportunities to get involved in your church's ministries and programs – and give them practical ways to use their God-given spiritual gifts. Provide ways for them to serve alongside adults and motivate them to get involved in work projects around the church. People are much more likely to continue in church if they have been actively involved themselves.

3. **Motivate them to give financially to the church.**

   I encourage youth workers to teach their students to give financially to the church. Most of today's teens have their own spending money. Their parents should be involved in this decision, of course, but teach them the discipline of giving financially to the Lord and to His church. It's hard to walk away from something after giving financially to it.

4. **Expose them to church business and key church leaders.**

I also believe it is a wise move to give teenagers some basic instruction on how their church works. Why do you have communion? Why do you baptize people? What is the purpose of church business meetings? These are vital questions and your kids should know the answers. It is also a good idea to give your students some exposure to the key leaders in your church – and that starts with the lead pastor or senior pastor. Don't forget he's their pastor, too. I encourage youth workers to invite elders, deacons, and other select church leaders to share their story with your students. Maybe our kids are leaving the church because they really don't understand it and how it works.

5. **Help them develop positive inter-generational relationships in the church.**

As I mention several other times in this book because it is so important, Dr. Chap Clark has said that if we want our kids to stay in the church after they graduate from high school, they will need personal relationships with five significant adults other than their parents.[1] How are you doing with that? These people can be various Godly adults in the church who build positive, Christ-honoring relationships with kids above-and-beyond our teams of "official" youth workers. They could be adult mentors, prayer-partners, Godly parents of other teens, work project leaders, or older adults who are genuinely interested in the next generation. I really believe that we are doing our students a disservice if we totally separate them from other generations in the church. We must think this through and begin to implement inter-generational connections if we want our youth to go on for God as adults.

Today's young people may be attracted to the energy, the connections with other Christian teenagers, the relationships with the team of Godly adults, and the fun of youth group; but if we are instilling more of a loyalty to youth group than we are to the overall church, there may come a time when they leave high school and walk away from church. We can avoid that scenario by building intentional connections for our students to the church as a whole.

CHAPTER 13

HOW CAN THE CHURCH BE A "FAMILY" FOR TODAY'S KIDS FROM HURTING AND DYSFUNCTIONAL HOUSEHOLDS?

In 1970 AUTHOR AND FUTURIST Alvin Toffler released his best-selling, *Future Shock*.[1] The book contained a series of his predictions about the future of industrial society. His list of future trends included the idea of "serial marriages" – which he described as "a pattern of successive marriages". He also suggested that society would soon introduce "temporary marriages" with no lifetime commitment and perhaps a predetermined ending point. There would be no divorce proceedings, the marriage would just be over, and the couple could move on.

I'm not sure how many of his projections have come true, but I am seeing evidence that the traditional family unit as we know it in this country is certainly going through a metamorphosis, and in many cases is struggling to survive.

Have We Arrived in a "Post-Family" Culture?

Statistically, fewer and fewer people are getting married – and those who are getting married are waiting later in life to do so. The number of children living with two married parents is decreasing significantly, and the number of single-parent, cohabiting, roommate, and same-sex households is growing exponentially.[2]

In fact, I just read that a group of university professors from around the world have collaborated on a report about the demise of marriage and the family, which is entitled, "The Rise of Post-Familialism: Humanity's Future." One reviewer made this observation, "We are witnessing a shift to a new social model. Increasingly, 'family' no longer serves as the central organizing feature of society. An unprecedented number of individuals… are choosing to eschew childbearing altogether and, often, marriage as well."[3]

The time has come where youth workers and other church and ministry leaders must realize that the "nuclear family" (where the family unit of dad, mom, and kids as the *nucleus* of society) is not the norm.

Today many, perhaps even most, kids will be from hurting, dysfunctional, and non-traditional households. In fact, as I quote elsewhere in this book, one well-known Christian leader recently made this pronouncement, "Churches that want to understand and serve teens and young adults should focus first on true household ministry, and not just family ministry."[4]

It would be great if church youth workers could serve alongside a team of committed and dedicated Christian parents who would collaborate with them to encourage kids to grow up and go on for God. That would be the ideal, but that is very likely not to happen in today's post-modern, post-Christian, post-church, and now "post-family" culture.

The Church Must be The Church.

Despite these seemingly dire cultural swings, the church, and youth ministry especially, is uniquely positioned by God to reach out and minister to today's post-family culture. The church being *the church* is the key. God established His church (Matthew 16:18) to make disciples (Matthew 28:19-20), to equip God's people to serve Him (Ephesians 4:11-16), to help believers to grow by teaching them the Scriptures (2 Timothy 3:16-17), and to operate as a family (Ephesians 2:19) by including everyone in what God is doing (1 Corinthians 12:12-26).

The Scriptures are clear that God wants His followers to function as a family. For example, believers in Christ are called Christ's "brother and sister" and "sons and daughters" (Matthew 12:49-50 and 2 Corinthians 6:18). The church is instructed to treat older people as if they were parents (1 Timothy 5:1-2). God Himself is called our Heavenly Father (Mark 14:36, Romans 8:15, and Galatians 4:6). Plus, those without a spouse or children have a "valued place and purpose in the family of faith"[5] (Matthew 19:1-12 and 1 Corinthians 7:32-35).

The important thing to remember is the need for the church to accept and include everyone, especially those marginalized by society, as part of God's family. This must include singles, elderly people, and "spiritual orphans" (those young people who do not have any spiritual influence from Godly adults),[6] among others.

God wants His church to be a place where human families are faithfully and actively involved in raising their children, surrounded by a community of Godly peers and influential adults. But He also wants His church to be a place that sincerely welcomes and involves those who are from hurting, dysfunctional, and non-traditional human households.

Here are some suggestions for church leaders to consider:

1. *Pray for kids.*

   I am convinced that the key to developing a family atmosphere in any church is to start with intentional and fervent prayer. Not only does God answer our prayers, but He also uses prayer to put a growing burden on the heart of the people praying for the ones who are the focus of their prayers.

   I would start with the oldest people in the church. Pastors and other church leaders should do everything they can to motivate older believers to pray specifically for young people. This simple step has the potential to revolutionize your church and is the most important, foundational step in helping your church move toward a true household or family of God (Ephesians 2:19).

   Seriously, this will work wonders in your church! Church leaders should do whatever they can to encourage the older generations in the church to pray specifically and individually for the church's young people. You will be amazed at how this simple step will help create a family atmosphere in your church.

2. *Develop an intentional mentoring ministry.*

   Another way to develop a family atmosphere in your church is to introduce an intentional, inter-generational mentoring ministry. The Apostle Paul instructed Titus to do the same thing in Titus

2:1-8. Older, Godly people can have an incredible impact on the lives of younger people in the church simply through a ministry of encouragement, exhortation, and training.

I am convinced that the best mentoring begins in the church foyer. Caring adults should take the initiative to greet and welcome younger people. It is amazing how these simple friendly conversations can grow into God-honoring, inter-generational connections in the church.

My wife and I are so thankful for the loving adults in our church who took our three children under their "spiritual" wings when they were growing up. These people included Sunday School teachers, youth workers, and other interested and caring adults who took the time to invest their interest, time, and energy into the lives of our kids who were growing up in that church.

I can visualize that scenario happening repeatedly in every church, where a team of Godly adults takes an active concern for every young person in the church. This is so important for kids from households that are struggling – and is important for kids from good, Christian homes as well. I believe that emerging generations are much more likely to stay actively involved in the church as they grow into adulthood if they have strong, personal relationships with caring older people in the church.

Of course, if your church is planning to implement an intentional mentoring ministry,[7] be sure to follow through on your child protection policies. It's a shame that churches need to think about the problem of predators and child abuse today, but it is crucial for every church to develop and publicly enforce these procedures and guidelines.

3. *Encourage good families to "adopt" needy and hurting kids.*

I wrote earlier about the importance of Godly adult mentors in the church, even for kids from solid Christian families. However, it is especially crucial for churches to make mentoring a practice with young people who are from hurting, dysfunctional, and non-traditional home situations. Churches should remember that the Scriptures teach the concept that the church is to be a "family", and that we are adopted (Romans 8:15 and Ephesians 2:19) into God's eternal household.

Too many of today's young people are from households without consistent spiritual role models. Yet, it is critically important for the church to provide Godly adults to function as patterns for kids without faithful parental examples. There is a great illustration of this very thing in the New Testament life of Timothy. He was from somewhat of a dysfunctional household (Acts 16:1), and yet the Apostle Paul, and probably other Godly adults, served as models (1 Timothy 1:2, 2 Timothy 3:10 and 14) of the Christian life for young Timothy to emulate and follow.

If the church is going to truly be what God wants it to be for kids from today's hurting households, Godly adults must be the accessible mentors and authentic models of what it means to live for the Lord that those young people will need. In other words, the church needs faithful adults who are willing to follow the Lord's example to essentially "adopt" hurting kids into their strong families.

4. *Build a culture of ministry and service.*

Another often-overlooked way of building a family atmosphere is to make serving the Lord a top priority. In fact, creating an intentional culture of service, where most of the church members and attendees are involved in specific avenues of ministry is probably *the* key to developing a family atmosphere in the church. It is through service that people feel included, keep their eyes off themselves, and feel the need to reach out to others. Teaching individuals and families to be actively involved in ministry and service is probably the most important thing a church can do to break down today's rampant and insidious attitudes of consumerism and self-centeredness.

It has been my experience that young people from hurting and dysfunctional households are more likely to feel accepted and included in a church that has a noticeable and obvious culture of ministry and service. They sense this culture because members of all ages reach out to them and minister to them when they first attend the church, and they tend to quickly develop a desire to serve others too because that is the overwhelming culture in the youth group and in the church as a whole.

Churches that intentionally function as a family are the churches that seem to make a lasting impact on their communities. I honestly believe that this will prove to be increasingly true as the looming *post-family* philosophy becomes more and more prevalent in our society.

SECTION 3

Parents and Households of Teenagers

CHAPTER 14

WHY MUST FAMILY MINISTRY (AS WE KNOW IT) CHANGE?

THE BIBLE IS CLEAR THAT there are two God-designed institutions that share the same God-ordained purpose. Both the local church and the Christian home are responsible to guide young people toward a lifetime of growth toward spiritual maturity. Once our kids come to Christ, because we are intentional about sharing the life-changing Good News with them (Romans 10:17), it is the Biblical responsibility of both the church and the family to help the next generation grow in spiritual maturity. (Ephesians 4:11-16 and Ephesians 6:1-4.)

Certainly, the Bible teaches that parents are the ones ultimately responsible to raise their kids in the "training and admonition of the Lord" (Ephesians 6:1-4), but likewise the church is responsible to equip or train "the saints for the work of ministry" so that the next generation "should no longer be children" and that they may "grow up in all things" in Christ (Ephesians 4:11-16).

Our kids' spiritual growth is the imperative mission of both institutions. Christian parents must raise their kids to follow Christ. Likewise, the basic mission of the church is to make disciples for a lifetime of growth toward spiritual maturity.

What is the relationship between these God-designed institutions?

Of course, the ideal scenario would be if most Christian parents loved the Lord and were committed and deliberate about raising their kids to grow up to go on for God. It would be fantastic if these Godly parents saw the importance of the local church in Scripture and were enthusiastic and loyal supporters of the church's youth and children's ministries.

But look around. Is that what we are seeing today?

If your community is anything like what is happening with national trends – that's not the norm.

I have observed four recent cultural trends that, without a doubt, will impact the way many churches minister to families:

1. *Young adults are dropping out of church.*

    We have all heard the statistics and I have cited them elsewhere in this book. Almost 70% of young adults who were once actively involved in church youth ministry walk away from God and the church following high school graduation. That trend is troubling enough on face value, but that departure has been true now for at least three generations (Generation X, Millennials, and Generation Z). The long-term ramification of this exodus from spiritual things is that both Generation X and Millennials are now parents, and many of them are raising their kids without consistent involvement in the church and the work of God in the world today.

2. *There is a lack of religious loyalty in today's culture.*

Recent church history has coined a new term, the "nones", to describe the most prevalent religious trend in today's American culture. Today's pastors and other church leaders are seeing this firsthand. Long gone are the days when the typical household in this country made church attendance and participation a top priority in their lives and schedules. One leading Christian research organization recently reported that a large number of people who claim to be believers habitually go to church services only one weekend per month – and yet claim that they are "regular" attenders.

3. *A post-Christian mindset dominates American culture.*

There is a dominant post-Christian philosophy in our world. Christianity is no longer the majority religious position in this country. History has taught us that the United States was founded on a Judeo-Christian ethic with a basic belief in Jesus Christ. However, most of today's youth workers and other church leaders are not seeing this to be true today. Post-modern secular thought is today's most prevalent philosophic trend. Most Christian leaders will admit that they are not seeing a pro-Christian and pro-church attitude in today's households. This mindset tends to govern how people look at the role of the church in contemporary culture. For example, many, many parents would rather their kids strive for a college degree that will lead to a well-paying job than they would have their kids sacrifice their schedules to attend church youth group functions.

4. *A changing household structure.*

> The following trends are significantly impacting this country's households: a rapidly decreasing number of children living with two married parents; an increasing number of single-parent homes; an increasing number of cohabiting, non-married parents; a growing number of households with single mothers; a growing number of same-sex households with children, and an increasing number of roommate households. In fact, some communities in this country are no longer referring to families and parents, but are instead using the terms "households" and "guardians or care-givers."

Pastors, youth pastors, and other church leaders are seeing these four cultural trends and are realizing that many of the people in their communities are no longer making church, church functions, and church programming a priority. Parents are choosing sports and other extracurricular activities over church attendance, and they push their kids to save money for college or other goals instead of encouraging them to commit to church or youth group.

It would be great if most Christian parents were committed to discipling their own kids toward lasting spiritual maturity, and it would be amazing if Christian parents themselves demonstrated a loyalty to the local church. But these are not the existing trends – and the way churches reach out to today's households must change as a result.

Please understand that I am not advocating a departure from the Scriptures in how church ministries should operate-just the opposite. I believe the church must "be the church" to reach people in today's post-Christian and post-church culture.

Can the church do it alone?

Yes, it is time for the church to be the church. It's time for churches to recommit to God's mission of reaching the world for Christ (Acts 1:8), of making disciples who live by God's instruction (Matthew 28:19-20), and of equipping God's people to serve Him (Ephesians 4:11-16).

God can and will continue to use His church to make a lasting difference in the world for eternity (Revelation 7:9). The church is God's idea, and it is His plan (Matthew 16:18).

It'd be great if all Christian parents were absolutely committed to raising their kids in the "training and admonition of the Lord" (Ephesians 6:1-4) and made the church a top priority for their kids. But most likely that is not what today's youth pastors are seeing.

May the Lord bless you as you seek to impact the next generation for eternity.

CHAPTER 15

WHAT ARE SOME SPECIFIC THINGS PARENTS CAN DO TO HELP THEIR KIDS GO ON FOR GOD?

THE BOOKS ARE FLYING OFF the presses in seemingly endless numbers. Frankly, I'm sick of hearing the statistics about the young adults who are dropping out of church. (I know, I know – I quoted some of those very stats earlier in this book!) But please, keep reading.

I want to start hearing about the kids who stayed in church. I want to hear the stories of Christian kids who grow up and go on for God. I want to hear about the successes of Godly, Christian parents who are proactively working with the church's youth leaders to develop strong, stable, and mature Christ-followers who, as young adults, decide to stay engaged in the church.

I know several young adults who are absolutely committed to Christ and His claims on their lives. Some of them are currently in college, others are in the military or work force, and many of them are currently living productive lives as God-honoring adults.

So, what can Christian parents do to help their children to grow up and go on for God? I'm convinced that we must look to the Scriptures for the answers! In the pages of the New Testament, we are told of some young people who grew up in the Biblical narrative and who continued to live for God long into their adult lives. One of those young men was Timothy. We meet him in Acts 16 as a young man growing up in church and we read his story throughout the Epistles, including Paul's last letter to him in 2 Timothy. There are many things in the Bible that we can learn about Timothy, but let's list some of the things his parents (especially his mother, Eunice - see 2 Timothy 1:5) did to honor the Lord and to help ensure that Timothy grew up to go on for God.

It's important to note that parenting is never a formula or a recipe. It doesn't work to frivolously think that a few quick ideas lead to spiritual success with our kids. However, if we look at the comprehensive principles that seemed to guide this family, we can take away some very practical advice for raising our own kids for God today.

1. A Consistent Lifestyle

> *"When I call to remembrance the genuine faith that is in you, which dwelt first in your grandmother Lois and your mother Eunice, and I am persuaded is in you also."* (2 Timothy 1:5)

Probably the most obvious thing that this family did right was Eunice's and Lois' consistent or authentic walk with God. The Bible calls their faith "unfeigned" (KJV) or un-faked faith! Timothy's mom and grandmother demonstrated a genuine relationship with God – and it impacted Timothy. Notice in this verse that Timothy also demonstrated a genuine faith. He grew up and went on for God – and that's what we want from our kids, too.

2. Communication of God's Word

"From childhood you have known the Holy Scriptures, which are able to make you wise for salvation through faith which is in Christ Jesus." (2 Timothy 3:15)

The second thing this family did right was that they made it a priority to communicate Biblical truth. Notice that from his earliest days, Timothy learned the Scriptures. The next two verses (2 Timothy 3:16-17) reveal that this strategy was much more than a rote memorization of the Text. He also learned that Biblical principles are "profitable" for life and that these principles lead to true spiritual maturity.

3. Collaboration with the Church

"Then he came to Derbe and Lystra. And behold, a certain disciple was there, named Timothy, the son of a certain Jewish woman who believed, but his father was Greek. He was well spoken of by the brethren who were at Lystra and Iconium. Paul wanted to have him go on with him…" (Acts 16:1-3)

There's another key element to their strategy that is worth identifying and that is their cooperation with the church to help develop Timothy's faith. Acts 16 identifies him as a "disciple", who as a young man already had a good testimony with the other believers. He also was personally recruited by the Apostle Paul to go along on this missionary journey. Acts 16:5 also expounds on the purpose of their ministry, "So the churches were strengthened in the faith and grew daily in numbers. " (NIV) Obviously, the church was a priority to young Timothy. He grew up in church and committed himself to a church-based ministry.

4. Concern for People and Culture

"Paul wanted to have him go on with him. And he took him and circumcised him because of the Jews who were in that region, for they all knew that his father was Greek." (Acts 16:3)

Acts 16 also presents an interesting scenario of Timothy's circumcision even though he was a Greek (see verse 1). He perhaps was willing to submit to this cultural ritual due to the cross-cultural background in his own family. This somewhat dysfunctional family environment undoubtedly produced a heart-felt concern for other people and a genuine sensitivity for others. Plus, his spiritual leaders know that his future ministry would probably target mostly Jewish people, and therefore they wanted Timothy to develop a tangible sensitivity for the people to whom he would minister.

5. Commitment to Ministry

"Paul wanted to have him go on with him. And he took him and circumcised him because of the Jews who were in that region, for they all knew that his father was Greek. And as they went through the cities, they delivered to them the decrees to keep, which were determined by the apostles and elders at Jerusalem. So the churches were strengthened in the faith, and increased in number daily." (Acts 16:3-5)

The final positive thing I'd like to identify from this family was their dedication to God's work. They were willing to allow their son to follow Paul along on this journey. Without any obvious hesitation on anyone's part, Timothy joined the missionary team and set off on what was the beginning of his call to vocational ministry.

Timothy was a young man who grew up and went on for God. The narrative of Scripture points out some identifiable things that helped in this process. Perhaps there is practical wisdom here for today's Christian families to implement into the fabric of raising their own kids.

CHAPTER 16

WHAT CAN THE CHURCH DO TO MINISTER TO INCREASINGLY DYSFUNCTIONAL HOUSEHOLDS?

W<small>E ALL UNDERSTAND THE VALUE</small> of a good home life. Statistics reveal that kids growing up in a consistent Christian home are much more likely to live for God and to be active in church when they become adults.[1] Of course, it would be fantastic if every kid in our youth group was from Godly and supportive families where Mom and Dad both love the Lord and are enthusiastic supporters of the church's youth ministry. But that's probably not what today's youth workers are seeing.

It is becoming increasingly clear that non-traditional and dysfunctional households are on the rise. Plus, due to youth sporting events and other extracurricular activities, more and more teenagers are probably missing church services and youth group meetings due to other priorities and involvements.

Those of us in youth ministry are serving in a time when much is being written and said about the importance of family ministry. However, since we are ministering in a post-Christian culture when the family unit is becoming less Christian and less involved in church programming, the time has come for the church to think through how to reach and disciple today's young people when their families do not support and maybe even do not attend the church.

Effective youth ministries through the next several years must consider how to reach this generation for Christ and how to disciple them toward long-time maturity in Him. The days where the "nuclear family"[2] (meaning the traditional family unit of Dad, Mom, and kids living under the same roof) being the nucleus or core of culture are gone. Current trends reveal that a growing number of American households no longer see church programming as an important and vital influence on their kids.

What can today's youth workers and other church leaders do to build thriving ministries in a culture where many kids are likely to not have a positive support-system from God-honoring parents at home?

Here are some practical suggestions that churches may be able to implement to minister to today's non-traditional and dysfunctional households.

Practical Suggestions to Consider

1. *Keep doing what youth ministry does well.*

   Historical youth ministry came to fruition with the goals of reaching kids for Christ, providing a place to develop positive peer relationships, and giving Godly adults the opportunity to build growing connections with young people. The current generation demands a return to those basic priorities for youth ministries.

2. *Present the Gospel - and creatively teach Biblical truth in a way that applies to life and answers life's tough questions.*

Today's households need good news - and we have THE "good news", the gospel of Jesus Christ. We also must reprioritize the creative presentation of Scripture so that our students see that it applies to their lives today and is God's source for them to find answers for their most difficult questions.

3. *Provide and promote a safe environment for kids.*

An increasing number of today's kids are growing up in difficult home situations with fractured relationships with their parents or guardians. Plus, daily news cycles are filled with accounts of adult predators who prey on vulnerable minors. More than ever churches must provide and then promote the safe environment they provide. Mandatory background checks and clearances are a required starting point; but churches must also intentionally build their reputations in the community as a place that loves and cares for kids.

4. *Offer quality spiritual resources.*

To have an effective and relevant presence in today's post-Christian culture, churches will need to position themselves as a positive repository of community-oriented resources. This will perhaps include making personal and family counseling available for today's struggling households, mentoring younger parents (see Titus 2:1-8), and using the church property, facilities, and budget more to meet the practical needs of the community.

5. *Connect with youth in their "world" and work with their over-scheduled lives.*

As I stated earlier, many youth workers are experiencing the trend that today's busy teenagers are not regularly attending youth group meetings or church services. Youth sports and other extracurricular activities, jobs, homework, and other commitments often come before church functions. Wise youth workers must make connections with teenagers outside of the church walls by attending *their* functions or by volunteering to serve somehow in the local schools. Instead of complaining about how busy today's kids are, maybe youth workers should rearrange our schedules to meet with kids in public places at other times – like maybe meeting them for coffee before school.

In these days of an increasing number of non-traditional, dysfunctional households, the church must commit to being "the church" – to do what God instructed the church to do. The statistics may tell us that the majority of kids who go on for God are from "good" homes, but church leaders must commit to reach young people for Christ by serving their communities, teaching and preaching the Word of God that relates to life today, and discipling kids to lasting maturity in Christ.

CHAPTER 17

HOW CAN CHURCHES REACH AND MINISTER TO "SPIRITUAL ORPHANS"?

THE RISE OF "SPIRITUAL ORPHANS" in our communities is a reflection of the true state of the family in today's American culture. I define them as those who have come to Christ, but who do not have the spiritual support system in place to grow in Him, or they are young people who do not have any Godly adult influences in their lives.

According to a recent national survey, almost 65% of Americans come to Christ between the ages of 4 and 14.[1] This is an important reality for any church to think through. If your children's ministry and student ministry are reaching young people for Christ, you undoubtedly have connections with spiritual orphans as a part of your ministry.

Plus, we are living in a culture today where most likely the "good Christian family" does not exist. According to recent statistics, more and more couples are living together without being married; the number of single-parent homes in the US is growing dramatically; there is a changing definition of "family" and there is a growing number of households in America that do not fit the classification of a "traditional" family; and the number of dysfunctional or fractured families is also increasing.[2]

Theologically, of course, there's no such thing as a spiritual orphan:

- God loves us so much that He sent His Son so that we can have a relationship with Him (John 3:16 and 1 John 4:10).
- Through Jesus Christ, we are adopted into God's family (Ephesians 1:4-5).
- Also, through a personal relationship with Christ, we become children of God, and are actually "heirs" of God (Romans 8:16-17).
- God Himself cares deeply for human orphans (Psalms 68:5).

However, in our present culture, the likelihood of us having the opportunity to minister to spiritual orphans is great. If we are seeing kids come to Christ, there will be several of them who are from households with very little Godly influence. This fact presents our ministries with a huge responsibility to help these young people become assimilated or integrated into the Christian community.

Ministering to "Spiritual Orphans"

Here are five strategic suggestions for your church to consider as you seek to reach out to the spiritual orphans in your community:

1. *Creatively and effectively present the Gospel.*

   We must never forget the truth of Romans 10:17, which says, "So then faith comes by hearing, and hearing by the word of God." God brings people into His family through His Word, and people grow in Christ through His Word. Because we are very likely to have a growing number of kids without any other spiritual influence in their lives, it will be imperative for us to make the clear communication of God's Word a top priority in our ministries.

2. *Provide Godly adult mentors.*

Most of today's students will respond positively to the influence of significant adults who care enough to build growing and healthy relationships with them. (Of course, it is imperative to build safeguards into our ministries including a well-defined and implemented "child protection policy".[3]) However, Godly mentors can provide a new layer of inter-generational relationships in your church's ministry to young people.[4] Many of the kids you reach for Christ today will be from households without the positive influence of significant adults. This is one of the reasons why it is so important for the church today to be inter-generational[5] in its ministry philosophy and programming.

3. *Show them God at work in the lives of their peers.*

One of the key advantages of any local church is the larger community of God's people. Positive peer pressure is so important for kids. If we can help spiritual orphans see God at work in and through the lives of other young people, they will begin to see this activity as the norm. Church youth ministry must never be dominated by fun-and-games, nor should they be entertainment-driven in their programming. Activities like that are important of course, but only as one of many methods to show the reality of Jesus Christ in life. All new believers need to see that other Christian can have fun, and that it is exciting to serve the Lord and to live out their faith in real-life situations.

4. *Help them connect with the total church.*

God designed His church to be inter-generational. The goal of student ministry is not participation in youth group. It must be that kids grow up and go on for God as adults.[6] We must grasp the fact that youth ministry was never designed as a terminal program where our students graduate from high school and then walk away from God's church. We can help connect them to "big church" through intentional involvement in serving, giving, worship, teaching and preaching, outreach, and other means of developing sweat equity. Young adults are much less likely to walk away from involvement in church when they become adults if they have been personally involved in church-wide activities when they were kids.

5. *Encourage good families to "adopt" spiritual orphans.*

It's interesting that the world grasps this idea and yet the church falls behind in implementing it. The general community where you live probably has programs for foster care services or mentoring programs where solid families take an active role in building relationships with kids from broken or dysfunctional households. Why shouldn't the church lead the way in this kind of ministry? Church leaders will probably need to paint the vision of how this could work. But the concept is sound - and it works. Good parents can be motivated to "adopt" kids who need to see what positive family relationships look like by including them in typical family activities like meals, sports, movie nights, etc.

May the Lord bless you as you seek to reach out to the "spiritual orphans" in your community.

CHAPTER 18

WHAT SHOULD YOUTH WORKERS DO WHEN PARENTS ARE NOT PARTNERS IN YOUR CHURCH'S YOUTH MINISTRY?

THE IDEAL SCENARIO FOR ANY youth pastor, of course, would be to have committed Christian parents as active, supportive, and true partners in the church's youth ministry. Christian parents are the ones most accountable for the spiritual growth and development of their own kids.

There are some parents to be sure who love what the church is doing with teenagers - and who appreciate the tangible benefits for their own teenagers to be enthusiastic participants in those functions. There are Christian parents out there, of course, who realize that the church is also responsible for the spiritual maturity of their kids.

Both God-ordained institutions, the Christian home and the local church, have the same God-given purpose to teach the life-changing Gospel of Jesus Christ and to train the next generation to grow into lasting spiritual maturity.

There certainly are some committed parents who see the importance of true spiritual growth in the lives of their kids who are vigorous contributors in that process at home, and who are absolutely committed to what the church youth ministry is trying to do as well. In fact, the statistics are overwhelmingly true that the students who grow up in those homes are the ones who grow up to live consistent Christian lives as adults themselves. That situation is exactly what God wants - and it is what works in real life.

But let's get real. The above-described scenario is getting harder and harder to find.

What do we do about it?

This is not the time for youth workers to throw up their hands in despair or uncertainty. It must be the time for church leaders everywhere to call God's people back to a true, radical commitment to Jesus Christ and His work in the world today.

But what should youth workers do considering the current trends?

1. *The church must be the church.*

   More than ever, it will be imperative for the church to truly be the church – and to concentrate exactly on what Christ designed His church to do. Today's local church youth ministries must clearly communicate the life-changing Gospel of Jesus Christ. Youth ministries and children's ministries alike should prayerfully consider a quick return to this movement's historical roots of developing relevant, creative, and energetic initiatives to share the Gospel with kids. This will require training students to share their faith and providing opportunities for evangelism to thrive.

2. *The church must fulfill Christ's mandate to make disciples.*

It is also time for churches to recommit to Christ's command to make disciples. Youth workers will also need to consider adjusting their programming approach to allow for more life-on-life discipleship like is described in 2 Timothy 2:2. Christ's ministry with His disciples did not look like an hourly program on Wednesday evenings and a few other scattered events. His ministry was real life as life happened and was a commitment of both the disciples and the Teacher.

3. **Churches must equip believers to serve Christ.**

The Bible is also clear that God's purpose for pastor-teachers is to "equip saints for the work of ministry" (Ephesians 4:12). This will demand inter-generational connections with the church as a whole, where church leaders and members understand and appreciate the importance of believers of all ages to be trained, motivated, and allowed to use their gifts and abilities in significant service for Christ.

Culture may be changing right before our eyes. It might be easy to respond with criticism and discouragement when parents do not support their church's youth ministry programs. But God is still on the throne and is still using His church to make an impact for eternity. He can and will continue to use youth workers to share the Gospel, to make disciples, and to equip God's people to serve Him with their lives.

Much of this article originally appeared: https://www.youthworkers. net/blog/when-parents-are-not-partners-in-youth-ministry-3039.htm.

CHAPTER 19

HOW DO PARENTS OF TEENAGERS APPROACH YOUTH MINISTRY?

L̲ET'S FACE IT; MANY YOUTH workers sometimes view parents as almost one of the *necessary evils* of youth ministry. A friend of mine took a survey a few years ago in his network of approximately 400 youth workers. He asked them to name the biggest concerns they faced in local church youth ministry. The most listed answer was "parents of teenagers."

Here are five basic ways that parents of teenagers approach youth ministry. It has been my experience that somewhere along the line all youth workers will face parents in each of the following categories:

1. **Protective**

   Undoubtedly, you've heard the phrase "Helicopter Parents" – those parents who "hover over their kids" and are overly-protective of them. One national cell phone carrier recently revealed that freshmen in college sometimes send and receive 11 text messages a day from their parents! The staff from Vision For

Youth noticed during our summer youth missions trips that many of the participating teens used their cell phones to call their parents almost every hour. It's true; we are ministering to a generation of hovering parents. My advice is to use this as an advantage and take every opportunity you can to communicate clearly and carefully to the parents of the teens involved in your ministry.

2. Afraid

Some parents are afraid, and they worry about the negative influences facing their kids. These parents look at their kids' peers as potentially harmful and manipulative. They also tend to see even the church youth ministry as a problem. The roots to this particular approach are often deeper than just surface negativity. There are some parents who seem to be pessimistic and critical about almost everything. Probably the best thing you can do to help these parents is to keep communicating to them the positive virtues and characteristics of the church and youth ministry.

3. Proud

Akin to the last approach is something I've seen growing over the past few years of my ministry. There are some parents who are so proud and arrogant that they feel as if they are the only ones who can have a positive influence in the lives of their kids. I've met some parents of teenagers who will not allow their kids to attend youth group or other youth ministry functions because they see those ministries as a problem. This group of parents looks at other Christian youth and even church youth workers as part of the problem, so they do everything they can to keep their kids with them in everything – including school and church activities. Again, I believe that communication is the key to ministering to this group of parents. Show them Biblical examples of the church in action and help them see the advantages of building other Godly people into the lives of their children.

4. **Idealistic**

Some other parents are quite idealistic. They think that everything will turn out okay in the end, so why worry about anything. These parents are often somewhat permissive and lenient with their kids. Plus, this group will often prove to be materialistic in getting their kids anything they want. I suspect that in most cases, their motives are good. They want their kids to grow up to be positive and constructive citizens; it's just that they try to smooth out all the feathers for their kids along the way. I have found that this group of parents may respond well if they see the positive aspects of youth ministry that includes actively serving the Lord and motivating students to enthusiastically share their faith.

5. **Engaged**

Praise the Lord for active, engaged parents. These are the parents who stay involved in the lives of their kids as they mature through adolescence and they are the ones who value the church's youth ministry and realize how important it is for the family and the church to work together to help kids grow in Christ and go on for Him as adults. This is the group of parents you should try to recruit to be a part of your team of youth workers. They will have a positive influence on their own kids and will often help minister to other teens as well. Praise God for engaged parents of teenagers!

Church youth workers are likely to encounter parents who fit in all five categories. Of course, it would be ideal if every parent was actively engaged in the lives of their teenagers. However, that's not likely to be the case. Some parents will be afraid. Some will be protective – and some will be proud and idealistic. The important response for youth workers is to be supportive of all parents and to seek to work with them for the long-term spiritual benefit of their teenagers.

CHAPTER 20

WHAT DO PARENTS OF TEENAGERS WANT FROM YOUTH MINISTRY?

Y OUTH MINISTRY IS REALLY A ministry to parents. As veteran youth worker Dewey Bertolini says, "Our ultimate effectiveness with teenagers may depend upon our concerted effort to gain an influence in the homes of our youth."[1] Sure, youth workers can have a real impact on the lives of impressionable youth, but our most effective long-term ministry may indeed be our entrance into the lives and hearts of parents.

We understand that God's Word gives the ultimate responsibility for raising children to parents, and especially fathers (see Ephesians 6:4 for example.) That's why a main focus of local church youth ministry should be upon equipping parents to be effective in how they raise their kids for the glory of God. However, most youth workers spend the majority of their time ministering to teenagers. The problem is that we sometimes fail to implement even the basic ingredients of an equipping ministry to the people most responsible for the spiritual maturity of our students: their parents.

The Lord has given my wife and me the opportunity to lead several seminars and workshops over the past few years for parents of teenagers and preteens. (This only means that "we're old"; our kids are grown up and are now adults.) This experience has convinced us that many parents are looking for the following five things from the church: communication, training, fellowship, encouragement and support, and resources. We have talked to hundreds of parents of teenagers and preteens in churches of various sizes across the country. These interviews give ample credence to our belief that every church should include these five priorities in its ministry to parents.

1. **Communication**

> Parents want to know what's going on in the youth ministry. What are you teaching their kids, and what are you doing with their kids? These are the imperative questions for any youth worker. Make sure that the parents know what you are doing. Well-known youth ministry author Doug Fields once quoted a parent from his youth ministry, "I would rather have over-communication than none at all. It shows leadership and it gives me confidence I know what is going on."[2]

> I encourage all youth workers to regularly communicate in every way possible to parents. Don't assume that the teens will get the information to their parents. This is your responsibility. Utilize your youth group website, e-mail, texting, newsletters, the church bulletin, announcements, phone calls, mailings, and all other means of communication at your disposal to get the necessary information to parents. I know several youth workers who schedule regular informational meetings with parents so that they do not have any excuse for not knowing what the youth ministry is doing.

2. **Training**

Parenting is a difficult task even for the best of parents. It seems ridiculous to me that churches don't make training and equipping for parents more of a priority. This responsibility is one of the most important tasks we face, and yet we often go into parenting so unprepared. It has also been reported that church growth guru George Barna has stated that parenting classes might be the most effective means of community outreach in contemporary culture.[3] It is no wonder, then, that so many parents of teenagers have told us that they wish their churches would provide specific means of training.

There is a very real tension here, though, because many church youth workers are younger than the parents of teenagers. I personally faced this apprehension as a young youth pastor, right out of college and trying to relate to the parents of teens and preteens in my church. I discovered that I could talk to them about the big picture of youth ministry without trying to state that I was some kind of expert on being a parent of teenagers. Frankly, I didn't have a clue how to be a parent back then, but I did encounter several teenagers in church each week, and I also made weekly visits to multiple high schools in our area. I couldn't tell them about how to raise their own kids, but I could share my own observations and conclusions about teenagers in general and the overall picture of youth culture.

I concluded that I couldn't provide specific training in how to be a parent of teenagers, but I could make other "experts" available to them. So, I utilized our senior pastor (he and his wife had grown kids) and other adults with parenting credibility in our church to lead parenting classes and workshops for younger parents. We also brought in outside parenting specialists for training and provided other training tools for our parents of teens and pre-teens to utilize on their own.

3. **Fellowship**

The third thing that parents need from church is fellowship. I believe that parents of teenagers desperately need fellowship and interaction with other parents of teenagers to show them that they're not in this alone. They also need fellowship with people from other age groups as well, especially with parents who have already raised their own children. Wise youth workers will help parents make these kinds of connections through various church programs and ministries.

I want to share another idea with you. Why not try planning some activities each year for parents and teenagers to attend together? Mark DeVries, the author of *Family-Based Youth Ministry*, touts this idea in his book. He writes, "I began with this rule of thumb: if it works with teenagers, try it with youth and parents together."[4] Maybe he is on to something.

4. **Encouragement and Support**

Parents need regular sources of encouragement and support. Ideas abound. The key here is to do everything you can within the youth ministry to show parents of teenagers that you appreciate the work they are doing in raising their kids for the Lord.

5. **Resources**

Finally, youth workers should do all they can to provide parents with some helpful resources and materials for parenting. These resources are plentiful today – check the internet and your local Christian bookstore. Perhaps you could create a library of sorts within your ministry for parents to check out books, websites, or other practical resources to help them with their kids. You'll need to be discerning about what kind of materials you provide for them. You should read or watch everything first and only then make those resources available that you would personally endorse or recommend. You may also want to involve the senior pastor in that process. Ask him to list some resources that he finds helpful for parents of teens and preteens.

As you gather resources for parents, don't forget the "people resources" that are a part of your church or community. What about doctors, police officers, child advocacy experts, lawyers, and counselors? Sometimes parents need these kinds of resources as well. Proverbs talks much about the "multitude of counselors." It is my experience that a church can make some crucial contacts for parents when they are going through difficult times with their kids.

It is very important for all youth workers to remember that they are not the parents of teenagers. Ultimately, parents are responsible for the spiritual maturity and well-being of their own teenagers. I am afraid that some youth workers inadvertently take on too much pressure by almost trying to be a parent to the students in the youth group. This isn't the best solution. Wise youth workers will work to add the above listed ingredients into the fiber of their youth ministries. This strategy will encourage parents and will help to get them on your side. We must not forget that the most effective youth ministry is undoubtedly a ministry that includes parents as a major focus.

SECTION 4

Utilizing Other Youth Workers

CHAPTER 21

WHAT ARE THE CHARACTERISTICS OF GREAT VOLUNTEER YOUTH WORKERS?

I HAVE KNOWN SOME AMAZING VOLUNTEER youth workers over the years. Some were energetic and enthusiastic extroverts. Others were quiet and thoughtful introverts.

I thank God for the Godly, faithful, "lay" youth workers who willingly share their time and their lives with kids. These people are the true heroes of youth ministry. They are impacting the lives of the next generation for eternity - and I know that God will bless them for their investment in the lives of teenagers.

I often tell volunteer youth workers not to beat themselves up for what they can't do. I encourage them to do what they *can do* to minister to kids, and to be faithful in doing those things over the long haul. There's not just one model or one version of volunteers. God can use a wide variety of models (some single, some married; some men, some women; and some young, some older), to impact teenagers for eternity.

Some volunteer youth workers are outstanding teachers who can creatively and effectively communicate the truth of God's Word. Other youth workers are energetic and talented worship leaders who are legitimately directing the hearts of their students to the Lord. Others are unbelievably talented in using technology, and some are really good at planning and organizing games and programs.

The individual skill sets are almost endless, but the most important characteristic of a great volunteer youth worker is that he or she loves the Lord, is actively living for Him, and is passionate about sharing the Lord Jesus Christ, in whatever way possible, with teenagers.

If you are a career youth pastor that is looking for other Godly adults to complete your team, or if you are a pastor serving in a smaller church and you need people to work with your church's teenagers, or if you are a volunteer youth worker yourself and need other adults to join you, the following list is for you.

Five Characteristics of Great Youth Workers

1. *They are living for the Lord.*

   As I mentioned briefly above, the most important characteristic of a great youth worker is that they love the Lord and are living consistently for Him. I'm not talking here about being a "super-Christian", but about being a Godly adult. They are someone who is faithfully living for Him and who desires to point others toward Jesus. It's not wise for churches to utilize adults as youth workers who are not genuinely living for Him.

2. *They are faithful and loyal.*

Great youth workers are those who are dependable and reliable. You can count on them to be there week-after-week, and even year-after-year. Kids need adult leaders that will be there for them. I've often said that one of the most important characteristics of a true servant of God is someone who will just "show up."

3. *They develop God-honoring relationships.*

Maybe the most practical and tangible characteristic of great volunteer youth workers is the ability to connect with kids and their parents. They work hard to build positive and God-honoring relationships. That is why a team of adult youth workers is so important. Each person will connect with a different variety of kids. Plus, don't forget that it takes time to develop relationships. Wise youth workers understand this truth and will proceed with caution and purpose to connect with kids.

4. *They are team players.*

Great youth workers understand that they are not "Lone Rangers". They are a part of a team, working together in and through the local church to accomplish God's work. They fulfill their role as teammates in the big picture of what God is doing. They understand that it "takes a church" to help students grow toward spiritual maturity, and they are willing to play their part to help accomplish that mission.

5. *They use the Bible consistently.*

> I know some volunteer youth workers who are amazing teachers – and I know some who aren't. Others are incredible in one-on-one situations – and are very effective as counselors and advisors. Some are talented communicators in large groups – and others are better in small groups. The important thing to remember is this: great youth workers use the Bible! Your students are looking for answers, and the job of youth workers is to show them that God's Word contains everything He wants us to know. Great youth workers get their students into the Word of God!

Anyone can be effectively used by God to influence teenagers for eternity. Some are young and others are older. Some are quiet and reserved, others are loud and enthusiastic. Some are single and others are married couples. The Lord can use a wide variety of youth workers with these characteristics to make a lasting impact in the lives of the next generation.

CHAPTER 22

NOW WHAT? PRACTICAL THOUGHTS FOR AGING YOUTH WORKERS

I AM A YOUTH PASTOR IN my late-60's. My hair and beard have been gray for several decades now and I can't play the guitar. I don't have a TikTok account and I've never played Fortnite. I'm too old to play tackle football with kids (or with anyone for that matter), and I hate staying up all night. I am enrolled in Medicare, and I have my AARP membership card.

However, I can say emphatically that I love kids and can't see myself doing anything else except working with emerging generations in a local church setting for absolutely as long as I can.

I know that I am way too old to play tackle football, but we should never get too old to minister to kids.

Believe me, I get it. My games in youth group can be lame, and my illustrations are sometimes old. I'm not the guy to lead worship for today's teenagers, and I am certainly not the person to lead all-nighters.

But, since most of the kids in our church are from dysfunctional, hurting, and broken households, they look at me almost as a grandpa. My wife and I minister to kids who may not have positive relationships with their parents, but they love their grandparents and respect them. Their grandparents are the ones who provide for them, who take care of them, and who encourage them.

So, maybe working with today's younger generations (like Gen Z and Generation Alpha) makes sense for older youth workers. Maybe it's time for older youth workers to refocus our ministries, renew our sense of calling, and allow kids (middle schoolers, high schoolers, and even young adults) to reinvigorate our ministries with today's young people.

Older youth workers can have amazingly effective ministries. Here are some things to think through:

1. **Reaffirm your call as you get older.**

   Has God called you to work with youth? If so, keep on doing it no matter how old you are. I don't think the call of God is age related.

2. **Stay relevant. Do your research. Stay connected.**

   How can you stay up on today's students? Maybe older people are inherently out-of-touch, and we'll have to work harder to learn all we can about today's youth and youth culture. The best way to learn about kids, by the way, is to spend time with kids!

3. **Concentrate on your strengths. You're not good at everything. Use what God is blessing.**

   Older youth workers probably are not the best game leaders, and most likely shouldn't be worship leaders at this stage of life. But they are really good at building interpersonal relationships, and they are probably ideal storytellers of what God has done over the years in their lives. And they probably know the Scriptures and can successfully teach God's Word to others.

4. **Recruit others to help you (and find people to do what is now hard for you to do). Build a team around you.**

Yeah, since we're not all good at everything, why not make a conscious effort to recruit other Godly adults in your church to work alongside you? Teams built with diversity are probably best suited to connect with the variety of kids in your group.

5. **Make much of relationships: with individual kids, with parents, and with others in the church.**

Older youth workers should be really good at developing healthy and positive relationships with individual kids. (Of course, churches will need to develop and enforce child protection policies for all adult workers!) Older youth workers also have the credibility to work with parents of teens too. Plus, they are likely to have the respect of other people in the church as well.

Friends, I can't tell you how thankful I am to still have the opportunity to work with kids and their families at this stage of my life. Our youth group doesn't play wild games and we don't entertain kids with the energetic music or creative videos that I have produced, but we love the Lord and we love kids and we want to see our students grow up to go on for God.

CHAPTER 23

WHAT ARE THE CULTURAL TRENDS YOUTH WORKERS WILL FACE?

REMEMBER THE FAMILIAR NARRATIVE IN Acts 17 when the Apostle Paul used his personal observations of the city of Athens as a springboard for an opportunity to share the Gospel with the philosophers that were gathered at the Areopagus?

Youth workers, let's apply this same action step as we make our final preparations for our youth groups this year. Let's use our own observations to identify some of the cultural trends that are facing our kids, and then use those trends as opportunities to reach out to them and the households they are from.

The big difference here, of course, is that Paul was a visitor in Athens – and we live in the communities in which we minister. But the same principles apply.

What's going on in your community? Do you read the local newspaper, or watch the local news to get a glimpse of what your community leaders are saying? Why not schedule an appointment with the principal or superintendent of schools where the kids from your church attend? Have you done a demographic study of the population trends in your area?

What are the trends and the needs of your community? What are you seeing? What are you observing that may provide you with greater opportunities to share the Gospel or to minister to kids and the households they are from?

In my research, I have identified the following cultural trends that I want to share with you here.

Some Cultural Trends Youth Workers Will Face:

1. *You will have kids in your group from a growing number of hurting households.*

   The demographic statistics in your community will probably prove this to be true. Members of Generation Z are from a rapidly increasing number of non-traditional, dysfunctional, and hurting households. It is very likely that several kids in your group will be products of hurting households.

2. *You will have to minister to kids who are from homes where church and religion are not that important.*

   Here's another trend that you will most likely face this year: church and church programs are not a top priority in the lives and schedules of many of the families who attend your church. Some researchers have recently reported that many families that claim to be followers of Christ only attend weekend church programs approximately once per month.

I've met with several youth pastors recently who have shared with me that it is a struggle for them to get their teenagers to regularly attend youth group. Other things, like sports and work, are more important to the students. It is becoming more likely that youth workers will have to find other creative means to connect with kids instead of thinking that today's teenagers will faithfully attend church and youth group.

3. *Several of the teens in your group will feel stressed, fearful, and uncertain.*

You have undoubtedly read about this in recent news reports, and if you have personal relationships with many kids, you will know that this trend is true. Perhaps it is a result of the Covid crisis, or maybe it was happening anyway, but many of today's youngest generations feel the stress of anxiety, fear, and uncertainty. Plus, the parents of your kids are facing these emotions too. This is a serious situation. The "mental health" of your young people is something very real. I'm thankful that we have the "living and powerful" Word of God that provides real answers for real-life situations!

4. *Some of the kids in your group are facing difficult "identify" issues.*

Here is another issue that youth workers will probably face this year. Today's kids are being bombarded with "identity" issues in the media, in school, and from a variety of other sources. Most likely you will have kids in your group who are struggling with distorted or unrealistic perceptions of themselves. Again, it's important to realize that our best resource to help kids with this is the truth of God's Word, and the demonstration of the unconditional love of Christ.

5. *Most of your students will need direction in finding their purpose in life.*

Kids probably have always struggled with this one. I know this was something that I had to work through way back when I was a teenager – but this is even more pronounced now. Your students will be thinking about the big "purpose" questions of life. "Why am I here?" "What am I supposed to accomplish?" "What should I do with my life?" You should teach your group about knowing and doing God's will, but you should also have personal conversations with each teenager to help them identify what God wants them to do with their life.

CHAPTER 24

HOW CAN YOUTH WORKERS ENCOURAGE OLDER PEOPLE TO CONNECT WITH YOUNG PEOPLE IN YOUR CHURCH?

I ALWAYS FEEL BAD WHEN I overhear some of the oldest people in the church complain to others about the style of music, the length of the sermon, or the fashion styles of the younger generations.

I wonder why this once active and vibrant demographic age group feels the need to express their frustration so openly as they get older.

Maybe it's because church leaders have just accepted and even unconsciously communicated the fact that as people get older, they often become increasingly negative, they have "had their day", and they need to just get out of the way so that younger leaders can have their turn.

The reality is probably much less dramatic and pronounced than my description. But I do think that many churches (maybe inadvertently, but perhaps intentionally too) have pushed older generations out to the proverbial pasture. Maybe older members feel like they have lost their voice and lost their influence, and so they need to share their concerns with other somewhat like minded people in personal cynical or pessimistic conversations.

I've wondered for years that maybe we could put a stop to this all-too-common scenario by developing and instituting a plan to deliberately and purposefully connect the generations in the church.

(I wrote a book about this idea a few years ago entitled, *"Inter-Generational Youth Ministry: Why a Balanced View of Connecting the Generations is Essential for the Church"*. You can obtain a copy at: https://www.youthministryquestions.com/book-store/inter-generational-youth-ministry. This book, however, is not really a youth ministry book. Instead, it presents practical and creative ways any church can effectively connect the generations.)

Friends, I am convinced that church leaders should prepare for the eventuality that people will get older, and may feel as if they are losing their influence. We can help them keep, or regain, their vital and vibrant ministries in the church by providing ways that they can have a growing voice and influence with younger people.

Here are a few practical ideas to consider:

1. **Encourage your church's oldest generations to pray specifically and individually for young people.**

   Take any opportunity you have to visit with your church's older people to ask them to specifically and intentionally pray for the young people in your church. Do whatever you can to facilitate this action step. Give them a list of names with copies of the kids' school pictures. One church made "baseball-card-size" info cards of every kid in the youth group to help that church's senior citizens pray specifically for their kids.

2. **Motivate your church's older people to develop friendly and growing relationships with younger people by utilizing space in the church foyer for simple, friendly greetings and conversations.**

Once your church's older people are praying specifically and individually for young people, ask them to introduce themselves to the young people in the public spaces of your church, most likely in the church foyer or in the church auditorium. Yes, the young people may, at first, think it's odd for the older people to greet them in this way. But ask the seniors to be persistent. In the long run, most young people would appreciate these simple, yet effective demonstrations of care and encouragement. One youth worker told me recently that their church asks the senior citizens to "show up and be nice" to kids. Honestly, this step goes a long way in connecting the generations.

3. **Ask your church's older people to utilize some of their resources to be generous and charitable with young people.**

I get it that these action steps may have just turned much harder and more difficult to implement. But I'm really not talking here about finances or other tangible means of charitable giving. In many cases today, older people have the available resources of their time, some of their energy, or their life skills and experiences that they can share with young people. Older people can certainly pray. They can send prayer notes or encouragement cards. They may be able to bake cookies or brownies. They can share their personal testimony with younger people. My mom invested in young people by showing some of the girls in her church how to make quilts. My mother-in-law used her musical skills to teach piano lessons. Really, the ideas are endless.

4. **Schedule simple, yet creative ways to connect the generations for social, fellowship events in your church.**

Your church can do this one easily. I know several churches that host enjoyable and beneficial inter-generational functions each year. I visited one church recently that scheduled simple games nights each year with round tables set up in the church's family room for table games, simple crafts, and fellowship. The ages were interspersed throughout the tables, and the youth group provided the refreshments, while the older people were encouraged to take the time to engage in personal and encouraging conversations.

5. **Plan opportunities for some of your church's oldest and most faithful members to share their story of God's faithfulness with the younger generations in your church.**

Today's younger generations love stories. Plus, your church undoubtedly has older members with lives of faithfulness to the Lord over several decades. Plan opportunities for some of your church's oldest members to meet with the younger people to share their story or testimony of how the Lord has worked in and through their lives. You will be amazed at how these simple times of connection will develop into growing and positive inter-generational relationships in your church.

These ideas are simple, yet they will not happen without church leaders actively getting involved in the process. This doesn't mean you have to be in charge to institute these ideas, however. You can use whatever influence you have, including your own initiative and your own persuasive abilities to ask some of your church's older generations to get involved.

You should also actively demonstrate to them that you sincerely care about them, that you want to hear their thoughts and concerns, and that you will do everything you can to encourage your church's younger generations to show their love and concern for older people.

CHAPTER 25

HOW DO YOU RECRUIT A TEAM OF GREAT YOUTH WORKERS?

No MATTER WHAT SIZE CHURCH you serve in – you can always use additional help in your youth ministry. Whether you are a full-time, career youth pastor or an adult volunteer worker, I'm positive that you could always use additional adult youth workers to assist you.

There are some very important reasons why every youth worker needs help. First, you cannot do everything yourself, and even if you do have the skill set to do everything, you shouldn't. Second, today's teenagers need several adult role models. It just makes sense to realize that other adults can make stronger personal connections with some in the group. And third, it is the team of other adult workers who will provide continuity in the ministry, both to the "big church" as a whole and to the teenagers in case there is a transition in the pastoral staff.

The real issue is how to recruit other qualified adults to work with you in your church's youth group. Here is a simple recruiting strategy which I recommend that you implement immediately into the fabric of your church's youth ministry.

1. **Make a list of the desired traits and abilities.**

This is the place to start in your search for additional adult youth workers. It's important to identify exactly what you are looking for in the adults who work with youth. I suggest that you get the church leadership team together and make a specific list of the qualities you expect. Undoubtedly the lead pastor has some specific characteristics in mind, as do the parents of teenagers, and other church leaders. It is essential for the leadership to be on the same page when it comes to the specific traits and abilities you are looking for in adult youth workers. Here are some possible things to consider. Are you looking for married couples or singles? Do all youth workers need to be members of your church? What skills or abilities should they possess? For instance, do they need to teach Sunday School, lead youth group meetings, organize games and activities, or lead a small group? Do they need administrative skills or is building relationships with individual teenagers more important? Don't forget to think about some practical things, such as if they need a specific class of driver's license to drive the church van. You'll also need to check with them about personal background checks and clearances.

It has been my personal experience that each church will have its own list of qualities that may or may not be important. You'll want to identify people who would make ideal youth workers – so be sure to take the time to start here. Make a specific list of the qualities you are looking for (see Chapter 23) – and then go on to the next step.

2. **Write down the names of potential youth workers.**

Once you have a list of the precise characteristics you are looking for, it is then important to make a list of the people in your church who possess those qualities. Many churches publish a church directory or other mechanism for listing all of the church members. Take some time to prayerfully work through that list or directory to identify which people hold those key traits and abilities. At this stage, just make the list. Once you have a list of people who potentially possess the qualities you are seeking you can then contact them.

It is also important that you review this list with the lead pastor, the elders, the deacons, or other church leaders. You want just the right people working with your youth, so go through this vital step. These church leaders may know more about the individuals on your list than you do. There is real wisdom in this "multitude of counselors" process. Youth workers should be experienced and dedicated. They should also be faithful and loyal. Of course, it is vitally important that these people do not possess any sinful habits that could disqualify them from effective youth ministry. That's why it is imperative that you obtain input from others. You want the most qualified people to work with your church's teenagers.

3. **Pray specifically for those people by name.**

Now that you have made this list of the people in your church who are qualified to be youth workers it is critically important that you bathe this entire process in specific and fervent prayer. Don't take this step lightly. The Lord Himself emphasized the importance of prayer in the recruiting process for laborers in

Luke 10:2, "Then He said to them, 'The harvest truly is great, but the laborers are few; therefore pray the Lord of the harvest to send out laborers into His harvest.'" Christ presented one way of securing new workers – prayer.

I can't emphasize this enough. If you need youth workers in your church, you must make prayer your highest priority. My advice is to get as many people as possible involved in this process. Remind people via the church website, the church's bulletin or announcement sheet, and by making public appeals to pray for this need. God can use this means of specific and heart-felt prayer to put a burden on the hearts of specific people for this strategic ministry.

But, I also highly suggest that the people involved in this process should pray specifically by name for the potential youth workers on your list. God works through prayer, and I know that He will specifically answer you as you call out to Him for youth workers.

4. **Approach the qualified people and ask them to consider being youth workers.**

I want to make it clear that I am not a fan of taking volunteers to serve as youth workers. I believe that the church leaders should approach the qualified people to ask them to pray specifically about being youth workers. It might be quite dangerous to accept volunteers as youth workers. It's sad to admit this, but we live in a day of predators and abuse. There might be carnal or sinful reasons why adults would volunteer to work with kids. Be careful about utilizing volunteers. There are some important guidelines about the selection of leaders or workers in Luke 9 and 10. Those who volunteered for service did not pan out. The

Lord specifically recruited and called those He wanted to follow Him. This passage lists some key principles about this subject. All of us would do well to study this account carefully.

You should approach those on your list who are qualified to serve as youth workers. Ask each of them to pray specifically about your need for youth workers and give them a deadline. In other words, you could talk to them about this need and ask them to pray specifically about it for a set period of time (for instance, about two weeks). Do not specifically ask them in this initial meeting to be youth workers – just ask them to pray about the need. At the end of that appointed time go back to them privately and ask them if they'd be willing to serve as a youth worker. If they agree to fulfill this responsibility you can then talk with them about the specific opportunities, job descriptions, training, and other specifics.

This simple strategy can be very effective. It's uncomplicated and efficient. May the Lord bless you and your church as you prayerfully identify qualified adults to serve along-side of you as youth workers.

SECTION 5

Youth Ministry Connections

CHAPTER 26

HOW CAN SENIOR CITIZENS MINISTER TO YOUNG PEOPLE IN YOUR CHURCH?

"Now also when I am old and grayheaded, O God, do not forsake me,
Until I declare Your strength to this generation,
Your power to everyone who is to come."
Psalm 71:18

ACCORDING TO THE US GOVERNMENT'S Health & Human Services Department, we live in a country with a dramatically increasing population of older people. At this moment, almost 40 million people in the United States are 65 years of age or older – and that number is expected to grow significantly over the next several years. It's definitely a ministry paradox to realize that this country's youth population is also growing at a considerable rate. Many churches are filled with a large number of young people alongside an escalating number of senior citizens.

Even though most of us have been raised believing there is a considerable "Generation Gap", I am absolutely convinced that the different generations in the church need each other and that both sides of the generational divide really want the same things in the church. Younger people and older people alike desire to serve and worship God in a local church environment that honors God, that teaches and preaches the life-changing Word of God, and that effectively reaches out to the unsaved and unchurched members of the surrounding community with the Gospel of Jesus Christ.

The Bible teaches the unity of the body of Christ (Ephesians 4:11-16) and that older people can and should mentor and encourage young people in the church (Titus 2:1-10). Today's young people need Godly and loving encouragement from the older people in the church – and current research points out that this generation of young people is very, very receptive to older people who care enough to develop growing relationships with young people.

Here are five simple things senior citizens can do to minister to younger people in church:

1. **Pray for them.**

   I highly encourage senior citizens to pray for their church's younger generations – specifically, by name! It's probably easy to obtain a list of their names from your church's youth workers. Encourage them to take each one to the Lord individually. God will begin to put a burden on their heart for them. They will be amazed at how external things fade away as they pray specifically for students and their spiritual growth. Once they have developed the habit of praying intentionally and individually FOR young people – then encourage them to take the opportunity to pray WITH them. You will be amazed at how receptive today's young people are for a time of special prayer with older people.

2. Encourage them.

It's also important for the older, established people in the church to actively and purposely encourage young people in their walk with God. Take the Biblical examples of Barnabas (Acts 11:23) and Onesiphorus (2 Timothy 1:16-18) to heart. They were exceptional encouragers. Today's young people hear so much criticism and negativity. Let's change that trend in the church. Imagine the positive influence senior citizens could have on your church's teenagers and college age young adults just by being a verbal encouragement to them. Ephesians 4:29 puts it this way, "Let no corrupt word proceed out of your mouth, but what is good for necessary edification, that it may impart grace to the hearers." Older people should take the initiative, even if it is simply an encouraging word or two to young people in the church foyer or hallway. Believe me, it will be greatly appreciated.

3. Share their story.

Today's youth love stories. Most of the recent blockbuster movies have been epic tales told as stories. God uses human interest, real-life accounts of real people to touch the hearts of others. I think this is the idea behind the truth in Psalm 78:1-8. Older generations were instructed to tell the next generation "the praises of the Lord. And His strength and His wonderful works that He has done...." This is so that, "They may set their hope in God, And not forget the works of God, But keep His commandments." This generation loves "God stories". Seniors should take every opportunity they can to share what God has done and is doing in and through their lives. Practical ideas abound. Invite young people over to your home and take the opportunity to share your testimony with them. Take a few young people out for coffee. Today's young people love to connect with older people. I strongly recommend that churches use this as a ministry advantage. This simple action step will help break down the "generation gap".

4. **Minister alongside them.**

It should be the standard norm in your church for each ministry position (ushers, Sunday School teachers, VBS leaders, etc.) to include a mentoring relationship with a younger person. Our churches must be intentional about becoming inter-generational. So, if you have any kind of ministry position at all in your church, why not invite a younger person to serve alongside you? Even if you are not a ministry leader you can still minister with teens by asking them to help you bake cookies to encourage someone in the church, or to go with you to visit a shut-in. The key is to demonstrate your desire to serve the Lord to emerging generations.

5. **Mentor them.**

I believe that every mature Christian in the church should have growing mentoring relationships with younger people. This is the Biblical pattern (see 1 Thessalonians 2:8 and Titus 2:1-8) and it should be replicated throughout our churches today. Recent studies have revealed that a vast majority of today's young people have indicated that they would appreciate an older mentor. Yet, most adults feel like they don't have time to do something like this. Friends, I have said for years that true mentoring is not necessarily a commitment of extra time. It is doing what you already do, just doing it with someone younger. The best mentoring takes place at church by the way. Begin this Sunday by building intentional, growing relationships with younger people.

It makes sense for older, spiritually mature people to be intentional about personally ministering to younger people in the church. Let's bridge that generation gap!

CHAPTER 27

HOW CAN YOUR YOUTH GROUP MINISTER TO YOUR CHURCH'S SENIOR CITIZENS?

"Let no one despise your youth, but be an example to the believers in word, in conduct, in love, in spirit, in faith, in purity."
1 Timothy 4:12

IF YOU COULD ONLY DO one thing to build your youth ministry's "street cred" in your church – start by ministering to your church's senior citizens! "Street cred" is contemporary slang for credibility, or commanding a level of respect. Honestly, friends – this is it! This may be the key to gaining respectability for the youth group in your church. Minister to the senior citizens! They have an incredible amount of influence in your church – and to have the senior citizens as fans of the youth ministry is a tremendous blessing.

In my last chapter I wrote about how the senior citizens can minister to youth. So, in the mode of "turnabout is fair play", here are some basic ideas for your church's teenagers to put into practice in trying to minister to the senior saints.

1. **Pray for them.**

It starts here. Motivate your group to pray for your church's older adults – by name! You can probably obtain a list from the church office or from the senior citizens Sunday School teacher. You'll probably need to remember that some of the key seniors may be "shut-ins" and unable to attend church very often. Don't forget these people should be the "heroes" in your church. They've earned your respect for their many, many years of living for the Lord. So, pray for them specifically and let them know that the teenagers are praying for them.

2. **Honor them.**

I've talked to several senior citizens recently and they feel somewhat "left out to pasture" or marginalized by the church. This ought not to be. They deserve honor – and it will be highly appreciated if your church's teenagers demonstrate their respect for these older adults. I know several youth groups that host dinners or other times of fellowship for seniors – and that is a great place to start. Let them know they are loved and respected by the emerging generations!

3. **Ask them.**

This is a simple idea, but it can be powerfully important. Give them a voice in the church. Your teenagers need to hear from them and need to hear their advice and counsel. There's one especially potent way that you can pull this off. Ask some of your church's Godly senior citizens to share their story or their testimony with the youth. A few years ago, I asked one of the oldest men in our church (a World War II veteran) to share his story with our youth group. He was a decorated war hero and yet he was scared to death by our teenagers. But, when he started telling his testimony, the kids were spellbound. You literally could have heard a pin drop in the room. This simple testimony helped our group connect with him and his wife. Strong relationships were developed out of this brief time together. It only makes sense to ask some of your church's Godly and respected senior citizens to share their story with your youth group.

4. **Use them.**

I am convinced that you could recruit some of these senior citizens to be youth leaders. Of course, they will all say, "I'm too old." No, the fact is that – people get too old to play tackle football, but they never get too old to minister to young people. I understand that in many cases it might not work for them to be full-fledged youth workers, but they can and should be involved. Ideas abound from helping with mailings and paperwork, to organizing them into an intentional prayer-warrior team. (Another key idea is to recruit them for work projects alongside teenagers. The mentoring effect will be incredible.) It will help them feel useful and needed.

5. **Help them.**

Here is one last way to minister to the senior citizens in your church. Offer to help them. Your group can help rake leaves, shovel snow, drive them to errands, pick up groceries for them, offer valet parking for them at church, and on-and-on. You will be amazed at how the seniors look positively at teenagers who are servants and who are helpful to them. This can help your group get their eyes off themselves and on onto the bigger picture of the body of Christ.

The Apostle Paul told Timothy that he could be an example to the believers in 1 Timothy 4:12. I highly encourage all youth workers to implement these simple ideas to help motivate your teenagers minister to the older adults in your church.

CHAPTER 28

HOW CAN YOU CONNECT THE GENERATIONS IN YOUR CHURCH?

Take a walk around the facilities of most traditional church buildings on Sunday mornings and notice where the various generations gather. The children are likely in one place. The teenagers meet in another place, and the adults gather somewhere else. In fact, in many churches the senior adults are isolated from other adults and get together by themselves in a completely different room.

Numerous churches segregate the generations, but the church didn't always function this way. Actually, the church probably adopted the custom because this is exactly what happens in the overall Western culture. The most obvious models for age-segregated programming are institutions like elementary and secondary schools, businesses with child labor laws, and juvenile detention centers. It has been society, and relatively recent practices of isolating young people from the larger culture, that has influenced church programming. (For an overview of the practice of separating the generations in an overall historical context, see Chapter 1 in my book, *Inter-Generational Youth Ministry: Why a Balanced View of Connecting the Generations is Essential for the Church*.)

In some ways, the habit of separating the generations makes sense. Children and teenagers learn differently than adults, and age-group specialists can concentrate on training people at certain ages and learning levels only. This approach is why many churches hire youth pastors and recruit trained children's workers.

The Bible gives credence for young people learning at different levels than adults. Passages like 1 Corinthians 13:11, Ephesians 4:14-15, and 1 John 2:12-14 seem to point out that young people are distinct from adults and that they learn quite differently than adults do. Recent scientific studies also substantiate the fact that teenagers learn differently than adults. Two veteran youth workers have recently researched this subject and have written extensively on this idea. You can learn more in Walt Mueller's article, "Inside the Teen Brain"[1] and Mark Oestreicher's book, *A Parent's Guide to Understanding Teenage Brains*.[2]

Christ Himself invested most of His time during His earthly ministry discipling young people. Most likely, all of Christ's disciples, except Peter (who was old enough to pay the required temple tax in Matthew 17:24-27 and who was already married, according to Luke 4:38, and perhaps Matthew or Levi (who was old enough to have a previously established business as a tax collector in Luke 5:27-32), were teenagers at the time when Christ called them to follow Him. Plus, the Apostle Paul also demonstrated a pattern to train young people when he discipled young men like John Mark and Timothy, both of whom were probably quite young when they met Paul.

Balance is Essential

There are some Biblical and practical benefits for an age-segregated approach to ministry. However, perhaps it's time for the church to swing the pendulum back toward a more balanced approach. Isolating young people exclusively from older generations has been proven by recent research to be one of the factors leading to a departure of young adults from the church following high school graduation. (For an overview of some of this research see "Conversation #3" in my book, *Going On For God: Encouraging the Next Generation to Grow Up and Go On For God*.) Emerging generations are much more likely to connect with the church as a whole if they have developed positive and growing relationships with Godly and caring adults as they progressed from childhood through their teenage years in the church.[3]

Not only does research support the fact that connecting the generations is a good idea, the Bible also makes it clear that an inter-generational approach to ministry is essential. One foundational passage for this imperative is Titus 2:1-8 where older people are explicitly instructed to "admonish" or encourage younger people.

The key is a balance in programming where churches provide peer ministry, like children's ministry and youth ministry for instance, alongside of inter-generational connections. Both approaches are presented and highlighted in Scripture. The problem has been that so many churches have ministry structures that are weighted toward segregating the generations.

Benefits of Inter-Generational Connections in the Church

A move toward balance begins by identifying some of the benefits of developing growing inter-generational connections in the church. These benefits include:

1. *The encouragement and mentoring from Godly older adults.*

   As mentioned above, Titus 2:1-8 sets the pattern for older people building mentoring connections with younger people to teach, exhort or encourage them in specific life-related matters. This text seems to assume that even then in the first century there was a "generation gap" in the church– but Paul instructed Titus to intentionally break down those generational barriers. Emerging generations desperately need instruction and shared wisdom from older people. Plus, this practice helps connect the generations in the church. Broad mentoring relationships throughout the church, like those described in this passage, are not likely to happen via age-segregated programming.

2. *Training for ministry and service from older adults.*

   Another key passage that contains valuable insights about connecting the generations in the church is 2 Timothy 3:1-17. Of course, the last two verses in that familiar passage talk about the importance of the Scriptures, but there are key principles and illustrations in the preceding verses that emphasize the importance of inter-generational relationships. Paul wrote in verse 10 that his disciple, Timothy, "carefully followed" the pattern of Paul's example. Verse 14 also contains instructions for Timothy to follow the teaching that he learned from significant and influential older mentors. In this passage Paul reminded Timothy about the training he received that helped prepare him for his future in ministry. Young people profit greatly from the hands-on training for ministry they can receive from people who have gone before them.

3. *Connections with the overall church.*

1 Thessalonians 1 and 2 also speaks to the importance of building growing inter-generational connections. In chapter 1, Paul mentions that the believers there in Thessalonica followed his example in that he followed the Lord (see verse 6). In chapter 2, the apostle presents a glimpse into what his ministry with the Thessalonian believers looked like. In 1 Thessalonians 2:8 he identifies two specific elements of his ministry with them: (1) "the Gospel", which was (and is) an advantage of older, more mature believers in the church, who can effectively share God's Word out of a life of maturity and wisdom; and (2) "our own lives", showing that another significant advantage of inter-generational ministry is that older people have the life experience that comes from faithfully living for the Lord and serving Him over the long haul. Younger people in the church can learn much from the invaluable insight that older people have from following the Lord for so many years.

4. *A variety of adult models.*

The narrative of young John Mark in Acts 12 and 13 contains an interesting illustration of the value of inter-generational connections in the church. This story takes place during a dark time for early Christianity. Church leaders were being martyred and others were imprisoned awaiting their certain death. During these days the text tells us that the church gathered for what must have been intense, all night prayer – and God dramatically answered their prayer by releasing the Apostle Peter from his incarceration under Herod. It's important to note in this chapter that the church's youth group may have been present for this time of prayer. The prayer meeting took place in the home of John Mark (see verse 12); and a young, servant girl, Rhoda answered the door (verses 13-15) when Peter showed up at their prayer gathering.

The conclusion of chapter 12 and beginning of chapter 13 begins the account of what became invaluable inter-generational connections for young John Mark when he was selected by older missionary leaders, Barnabas & Saul (soon to be the Apostle Paul) to accompany them on the church's very first mission trip.

Of course, there is much more to this story, but this young man, who grew up in the church that met in his mother's house (see Acts 12:12), was mentored and discipled by some of the leading influencers in the early church—Peter, Barnabas, and Paul. It's no wonder that John Mark, who went through some struggles along the way, ended up being greatly used by God. He was the human author of the Gospel of Mark and the Apostle Paul referred to him as being "useful... for ministry" in 2 Timothy 4:11.

As mentioned earlier, separating the generations may have some merit and there are examples in the Scriptures of times when that model was effective and important. However, it's also essential for young people to develop healthy and growing connections with Godly older believers in the church. Balancing these two approaches is the key. Building inter-generational connections alongside peer ministry is crucial for the church.

This originally appeared: https://www.crosswalk.com/church/pastors-or-leadership/is-your-church-missing-out-on-connecting-the-generations.html.

SECTION 6

Ministering to Your Church's Young Adults

CHAPTER 29

HOW CAN YOUR CHURCH MINISTER TO YOUNG ADULTS?

Current research has revealed that ministering to college age young adults may be the weakest area of ministry in many, many local churches. We need to fix that trend immediately!

I am convinced that any church can and should minister to young adults by implementing a few proactive and simple strategies.

However, before I list those ideas, I must emphasize the fact that a ministry to this age group requires a commitment to do it. Many churches see high school kids leave the church following active involvement in youth group without tracking them to see where or if they are going to church or if they are even living for the Lord.

We must change this trend and invest in this "missing generation" in our church. A ministry to this strategic age group begins with a commitment of people resources. In other words, churches must decide to make college-age, young adult ministry a priority.

Here are some ideas on how your church can minister to this important demographic:

1. **Start by developing an opportunity to teach them God's Word!**

   This really is a simple place to start. Does your church have a Sunday School class for college-age young adults? If not, why not start one right away? Even your recent high school graduates need a place to study God's Word following their involvement in the youth group. Recruit significant, Godly adults in your church to lead this new ministry – and remember that this current generation is not looking for a revision of what they got in youth ministry. College-age students want to be treated as adults; in fact, many of them may be enrolled in high-academic college or university majors. It doesn't make sense for the church to give "fluff" to this age group when they are craving serious and important truth!

   If your church does not have the resources for a traditional Sunday School class, you could develop a regular time of Bible study for them instead. This age group needs Biblical answers that counter the various secular world views they are hearing in college. So, a teaching ministry is the place to start!

2. **Provide Godly older mentors to build growing, personal relationships with this age group.**

   This age group needs older people! The church can and should provide Godly older mentors for this generation of emerging young adults. So many college-age para-church organizations tend to separate young adults from the church by gathering groups of peers together on college or university campuses. Friends, this is a mistake. This demographic cohort desperately needs the church. The church can provide the human resources of a "family" of older adults who are willing to develop growing relationships and connections with college-age young adults. Encourage and teach your church's older adults to take the time to build personal relationships with younger adults.

3. **Supply opportunities for this age group to have fellowship.**

Friends are the lifeline for this age group. That's another reason why churches should "do something" for young adults. The church can and should provide real fellowship – with other members of this age group and with other ages. It's a shame, in some ways, that college and university students tend to develop their friends outside of the church. This generation is not looking for a series of "youth group games" or activities. A ministry to college-age young adults should look differently than that. Fellowship for this age group will probably feature hanging out around a cup of coffee instead of taking the members to the nearest amusement park.

4. **Give them leadership opportunities in the group and in your church as a whole.**

One of the most effective ways to offer something for this age group is to give them some specific leadership duties within the group – and within the greater structure of the entire church. In other words, give them something to do, with real responsibilities. This generation can lead Bible studies, organize events, and will have influence on their peers. They are no longer teenagers – they are emerging adults. Give them leadership opportunities and work to train them for future positions of leadership in the church.

5. **Offer resources to help this age group become involved.**

A very effective way to minister to this age group is for the church to supply resources for this generation that is in so much transition. Mentoring is one way to do that, but there is a vast variety of ways that a church could minister to college-agers. One church (located near a major university) hosts a meal for college students every Sunday afternoon. Another church provides transportation to and from the nearby college campuses. My home church recruited a team of families to host college-age students in their homes on Sunday afternoons. The point is that every local church has a supply of resources that could be utilized to minister to this age group. Ideas are almost endless.

These simple ideas do not do justice to this important aspect of church programming. However, it is a shame for churches to do nothing – especially when the number one time people walk away from church is immediately following high school. It's time to do something – and the above listed ideas are where to start.

CHAPTER 30

HOW CAN YOUR CHURCH CONTINUE MINISTERING TO YOUR YOUNG ADULTS WHO ARE AWAY AT COLLEGE?

I LIVE IN A COLLEGE TOWN. Just this week I met a young girl who will be attending college here this fall, so I asked her if anyone from her home church recommended a good church to her while she completes her studies. She replied that no one from her home church, including her parents or pastors, had said anything to her about finding a good church in the town where she is attending college. Of course, I suggested that she should try our church; but that conversation left me wondering.

Are pastors and youth pastors talking to their church's graduating high school seniors about getting plugged in to a good church while they are away from home attending college?

Here are five practical suggestions for ministering to your church's college students who are away from your church while they are in college.

1. **Encourage your church's college students to find a good church immediately when they arrive on campus!**

    If nothing else, take the time to talk to the college students from your church who are away from home about finding a good, Bible-preaching church in the town where they are attending school. You might also want to take the time to investigate the churches in the area where your students are living to make informed recommendations to them. This will not take a long time with the wealth of information available on the Internet. Make sure your young adults are plugged in to a good church nearby the college or university they are attending. Believe me, this is also important if your students are attending a Christian college or even a Bible college. Experts on this age group are saying that college-age habits are usually formed within the first two weeks they are away from home; so, this suggestion is very important for their spiritual growth and development while they are away in college.

2. **Stay in touch with your church's college students encouraging them in their walk with God.**

    Your church's high school graduates are likely to leave home following their time in high school to pursue their academic or career goals. Make sure you know their mailing address, e-mail address, and cell phone number so that you can stay in touch with them while they are away in college. Put it on your personal schedule to send them an e-mail or a text message just to find out how they are doing in college and to let them know that people from their home church are praying regularly for them.

3. **Send them a "love gift" from home within 2 weeks of when they arrive on campus.**

   Make sure your church sends them a *care package* (home-made chocolate chip cookies are a must for college students!) within a couple of weeks of when they start their education. You might also want to send them a gift card for a free pizza. Why don't you recruit a team of church people to handle this important detail? There's nothing like the encouragement from receiving a love gift from people back at home.

4. **Suggest ways they can stay connected with their home church while they are away at college.**

   College students often feel out-of-touch while they are away from their home church. Perhaps it would be a good idea to send each of them your church's weekly church bulletin and prayer request list. Put this simple practice on a *tickler file* as a reminder to send them this information on a regular basis.

5. **Recruit a team of people in your church to pray specifically for those students while they are in college.**

   I can't tell you how important it is for today's college students to know that caring people back home are praying regularly for them while they are away at school. Put together a complete list of the young adults from your church who are away in college (and in the military, for that matter) and add them to your church's prayer list. Then make sure you remind your church people to pray for them regularly and faithfully. This simple act of prayer will be a real source of encouragement to your church's students who are studying away from home.

Please don't forget that these students are still your church's young people. Your church has invested so much in their lives during their formative years as children and youth. Don't forget about them while they are away in college!

SECTION 7

Other Important Youth Ministry Topics

CHAPTER 31

HOW CAN SMALL YOUTH GROUPS MAKE A BIG IMPACT?

A RECENT REPORT STATED THAT THE average church in America has about 75 people, 4 of whom are teenagers.[1] I don't know if that description fits your church, but the report shows that the typical church is nowhere near the size of a megachurch.

Large churches seem to get all the attention, but let's face it; most churches do not have the facilities, budget, or number of people to garner a great deal of interest from anyone other than the regular members or attendees. Therefore, it's quite easy for pastors and other leaders in smaller churches to get discouraged when some of their people seem to be attracted to the larger megachurches in their communities.

In my opinion, there seems to be a growing church insecurity about having a small congregation. A friend of mine has repeatedly stated, "Every small church is trying to get bigger, and every large church is trying to get smaller." He is obviously talking about the trend today toward small-group ministries. I admit that I have some cautions about small groups, and I advise churches to implement some guidelines into the organization of their small groups; but for the most part, I am a fan of small groups in the local church. There's a great deal of good that can come from a small-group ministry.

I grew up in a small town. My family attended a small church, and I was active in a small youth group. Over the years of my ministry, I have visited or preached in a variety of churches of all sizes. I have also talked to several volunteer youth workers in churches with very small youth groups or youth Sunday School classes.

Those experiences have given me the following perspective of the advantages of small church youth ministry.

1. **Make much of people, not programs.**

   The biggest advantage of being in a small church is that we can emphasize people over programs. Somehow, we must learn that it doesn't take an organized structure to do real ministry. Effective ministry can happen in our kitchens around a cup of coffee or in our living rooms with our feet propped up on the coffee table.

   I am becoming increasingly convinced that today's students are much more impressed by adults who genuinely care about them than they are with overly organized and structured programs. Don't get me wrong, I see value in organization and structure. However, smaller churches have a real advantage over bigger churches in the development of close relationships.

   If you are a youth worker in a small church, you can have everyone over to your house for dinner, or take the whole class out for McDonald's milkshakes without taking out a second mortgage or robbing a bank. If you only have a handful of students in your group, you can probably get out to their high school football games or concerts. You can remember everybody's birthdays, and you can pray for each one specifically each day. You can show them how to do their own personal devotions and you can answer specific life-related questions. You can become their friend and not just another acquaintance from church. One of the great advantages of serving in a small church is the ability to make much of people instead of programs.

2. **Stress relationships, not rooms.**

It seems that the modern church is more interested in building buildings than building lives. That statement may sound a bit sarcastic, but it is a mistake for churches to view their buildings as a priority over their ministries in the lives of people.

A pastor friend of mine recently experienced a fire in his church building that practically destroyed the facility. Even though insurance paid for the reconstruction of their building, he said this to me during the process: "I'd almost like to do without our building permanently. [Without the building] our people were closer, the fellowship seemed to be more genuine, and the church seemed to be real." Perhaps he was right. Maybe our elaborate buildings and facilities sometimes get in the way of real ministry.

I've had many youth workers over the years ask me about their youth rooms or Sunday School classrooms. Ideal facilities would be nice, but most churches I know of do not have the money or budget to build "perfect" youth meeting rooms. In fact, I have had occasions where I taught teenagers in church buses, in gymnasiums, in basements where I couldn't stand up straight, and in closets under the stairs.

I really don't think that Christ would have been overly concerned with PowerPoint, smart boards, or sound systems. He may have utilized those things, but I'm sure that His focus would have been to develop strong interpersonal relationships with His students. Sure, He made use of visual aids. He wrote in the dirt on the ground and referenced objects in nature to visualize the truth He was teaching. But mostly He concentrated on people. That seems like a good idea for ministry with teenagers today.

3. **Build trust instead of technology.**

I certainly enjoy modern technology. I love my laptop and carry my iPhone and iPad religiously. My son wrote me a note recently that stated, "You are the only Dad who has cooler toys than his kids." Yep, I admit that I am a collector of technological toys. But let's all be careful not to let our electronic gadgets isolate us from people.

I am old enough to remember the days when "Walkmans" were the great evil in youth ministry. Youth workers then feared that kids on the bus who listened to that "cutting edge" technology would drown out conversations with other people. These workers made rules that wouldn't let kids bring those old cassette tape players on youth trips. Remember those days? Now we are all hearing that modern technology actually helps kids connect with each other. One news organization recently reported that today's teenagers would be willing to do without almost anything they owned, except for their cell phones.[2] I'm sure that technology can help us stay connected to our students, but let's be careful not to send text messages or emails to kids when we should be talking to them in person. I think we should utilize every means possible to stay in touch with teenagers, but let's be sure to include spending time with them individually as well. You can do that very well in a smaller church.

4. **Emphasize mentoring over methods.**

Somehow it seems that contemporary youth ministry has become carried away with "methods". "How to" has become the latest and greatest trend. It is imperative for all of us to work on our creativity and imagination. All of us should get better at implementing creative Bible learning and imaginative methods in our teaching. But we should never sacrifice Biblical truth at the altar of student involvement or interaction. It also seems like today's youth workers are constantly looking for the next "what works" method for ministry. Countless conferences and seminars tout the latest and greatest technique for youth ministry. These methods are fine, but we must never forget that real, Biblical ministry should focus on the spiritual practices of basic discipleship (2 Timothy 2:2) and mentoring (1 Thessalonians 2:8).

Mentoring is a concept that must be intentionally implemented into the fabric of our ministries. It can be an effective way to connect the various generations with each other in our churches. The fundamental idea of mentoring is that caring, Godly adults should take the initiative to develop intentional growing relationships with young people. In other words, we must encourage adults to do what they normally do, just to do it with students. For instance, my mom was a very talented quilt maker. She had a very effective ministry showing young ladies in her church how to quilt. My mother-in-law loved music. She took some of the young girls in her church to piano recitals and concerts. That's the concept so aptly described in Titus 2:1-8.

Older men and older women can have an incredible mentoring ministry by spending time with teenagers.

5. Train, don't just "teach."

My last suggestion may seem strange. I believe in teaching and have spent most of my life involved in various teaching endeavors. But we must emphasize training or equipping, not just the verbal presentation of facts. Our ministries must feature training, not just lectures. I also believe in the importance of preaching. However, my focus here is on the significance of true education – which is making sure that our students learn.

Christianity must impact the lifestyles of our students. That's why the truth of James 1:22 ("be doers of the word, and not hearers only") is so critical for today's culture. Our students need to see how Biblical principles relate to life today. I love the account in Luke 24 of Christ's post-resurrection appearance to some of His disciples. Verse 32 presents this interesting question, "Did not our heart burn within us, while He talked with us on the road, and while He opened the Scriptures to us?" Christ taught them the Bible while He walked with them through their journey. Perhaps that is an apt description of what real ministry is all about: showing students that God's Word relates to life!

May God bless you as you minister to today's students, even in small churches.

CHAPTER 32

HOW CAN CHURCHES "GEAR UP" FOR THEIR FALL YOUTH PROGRAM?

"DRIVERS, START YOUR ENGINES!"

Our "neck of the woods" is especially busy and bustling with excitement and energy one week each year[1] as the *NASCAR* universe descends on northeastern Pennsylvania for its race at Pocono Raceway. Every hotel room for miles around is full and the highways are jammed with race fans crowding into "Long Pond" for this annual event.

It's always interesting to watch the sleepy countryside of this region's Pocono and Endless Mountains come alive in preparation for the huge onslaught of NASCAR enthusiasts. There are car races each weekend somewhere during the summer, but on one particular weekend our area plays host, and Pennsylvanians work hard to get ready for the big race.

Fall can be one of those "race weekends" for church youth workers. It is the time for our students to head back to school, which means that graduating seniors have left for college or to pursue their careers, and a new group of pre-teens will transition into the youth group. Fall is the ideal time for youth workers to "gear up", to re-energize their ministries with a new theme, a new logo or decorations, and perhaps a new team of volunteer youth workers.

Here are five important suggestions that may help you prepare for your renewed push this fall:

1. **Make the time for individual appointments with incoming students.**

   If you haven't done this yet, take the time to meet individually with your group's incoming new students. I highly recommend that you take the opportunity each summer to meet personally with each young person who is transitioning into your youth group. Of course, be sure that you have implemented your church child protection policies into these meetings. You should also consider connecting with the student's parents as well, and you'll want to include your spouse or another youth worker as you meet with kids of the opposite gender. These appointments would be the ideal time to welcome individual kids into the group and to share your vision for the church's youth ministry with them. This would also be the perfect time to talk to each teen about how they came to Christ and about their personal walk with God. Of course, it only makes sense in larger groups to divide up these appointments with other key youth workers.

2. **Make the effort for a renewed push for your new fall program.**

   Someone once said, "If it's important, it's worth talking about." I am a firm believer in promotion and advertising, but not in a "consumerist" or carnal way. It's a good idea to promote your fall program to create energy and enthusiasm for what you are trying to accomplish this year in your ministry. Some youth workers repaint or redecorate the youth room each year, while others send out creative promotional pieces featuring the new theme or a new logo. The important thing to remember is that what you are trying to do to minister and to reach out to kids is important. Treat it as if it is important because it is important.

3. **Make sure to communicate your plans to the parents of teenagers.**

Work hard right now to develop a plan to regularly communicate the details of your fall program to the parents of teenagers. Send out emails, develop a new push for your social media pages, put announcements in the church bulletins, obtain the parents cell phone numbers and send them text messages, etc. Do whatever you can to put the most pertinent information into the hands of parents. Let's face it, they will never really be on your side unless they know what is going on.

4. **Make the commitment to see how your plans fit in with the overall plans of the church.**

Take the time to meet with your lead pastor or senior pastor to go over your plans with him. It will help him to know what is going on and it will help you see what his thoughts are for the big picture of your church's ministry. Be proactive, be prepared, and be willing to tweak your ideas to fit in with his philosophy of what he wants for the church.

5. **Make sure to cover your fall program in prayer!**

Now's the time to commit everything you want to do this fall to the Lord and to ask for His blessing! It's also imperative that you meet with the other members of your youth ministry's leadership team to encourage them to pray specifically for the teens. I also encourage youth workers to meet with your church's oldest adults to ask them to pray specifically and individually for the students. Do whatever you can to recruit prayer warriors for the youth ministry!

Thanks for reading. It's time to gear up for fall!

CHAPTER 33

WHERE IS YOUTH MINISTRY HEADED?

I AM CURRENTLY IN MY LATE sixties, and am still a youth pastor. My wife and I started working with teenagers in the mid-1970s, and I have been actively involved in youth ministry in a wide variety of ways ever since. That means I have personally experienced some of the major youth ministry trends in the last several decades.

Although I wasn't around then, contemporary youth ministry can be traced back to the 1940s when visionary and highly-motivated leaders observed the looming youth culture and developed creative and culturally-relevant methods to communicate the Gospel to the next generation. The Lord used people like Jim Rayburn, Torrey Johnson, Jack Wyrtzen, and Percy Crawford and other entrepreneurial trailblazers to launch creative organizations and programs to reach kids for Christ.

Other innovative leaders have stood on their historical shoulders in the eight decades since. These youth ministry giants include people like Henrietta Mears, Lance Latham and Art Rorheim, Mike Yaconelli and Wayne Rice, Thom Schultz, Dann Spader, and Paul Fleischmann.

I get that not all readers will recognize the names listed here. But each person mentioned paved the way for today's youth workers.

If you are interested in the reading more about the history of youth ministry, I would recommend the following works: *When God Shows Up: A History of Protestant Youth Ministry in America* by Mark Senter III, *Reinventing Youth Ministry Again* by Wayne Rice, and *A Biblical Theology of Youth Ministry* by Mike McGarry.

Youth ministry today is going through a much-needed metamorphosis. Every strategy and methodology must be evaluated in the light of Scripture. Certainly, the discipline of youth ministry can be commended for its innovation, energy, and relevancy. Most youth workers understand that they must be students of culture and its influence on emerging generations to effectively impact the lives of teenagers. We can also applaud youth workers for learning how to communicate well to each succeeding generation of young people. Of course, it is imperative that theology drives methodology.

The much-reported church departure rate of young adults following their active involvement in church youth groups is cited by some as a legitimate criticism of youth ministry. Others blame youth ministry for its "segregation" of teenagers from other generations, and some accuse youth ministry of featuring too much entertainment instead of concentrating on the preaching and teaching of the Bible.

Youth ministry (as we know it) is at a crossroads. As someone who has spent most of my ministry life actively involved in youth ministry, here are some of my recent observations.

1. **Youth ministry has moved to the local church.**

   Early youth ministries were mainly parachurch driven, and it took some time for the church to catch up. Organizations like Youth for Christ, Word of Life, and Young Life organized city-wide rallies, and school or home-based clubs. Lately, church-based youth pastors have been the driving force for creativity in youth ministry. Sure, parachurch organizations still exist and do meaningful ministry, but many of today's youth workers understand that God's plan for today focuses on getting young people involved in the local church.

2. **Youth ministry is concentrating on discipleship.**

   Another positive development in youth ministry has been the movement toward prioritizing discipleship. By and large, youth workers have identified the mandate of the Great Commission in Matthew 28:19 to "make disciples", and they are making that the priority in their ministries. Examples include the current emphasis on small groups and the creation of discipleship groups within the structure of many youth ministries.

3. **Youth ministry is emphasizing preaching & the importance of Biblical literacy.**

   As youth ministry evolved from the early days of evangelistic youth rallies in large stadiums, to "clubs" meetings in homes, to "fun and games" approaches, it has always been known for its obsession with cultural relevance. Visionary youth leaders had the reputation for being cool and edgy. They had the ability to attract kids through their programming and "pied piper" personalities. But many eventually realized that teenagers need more than entertainment and programming. They need to hear, study, and learn the Word of God. They need the life and grace that only comes through faith in the Gospel of Jesus Christ.

4. **Youth ministry is becoming inter-generational.**

Historical youth ministry has been characterized by an emphasis on adolescents to the exclusion of other age groups in the church. Recent developments in youth ministry indicate that churches are beginning to realize it is not wise to exclusively separate teenagers from the overall life of the church. This approach encourages churches to view teenagers as valuable family members. I wrote on this subject in my book, *Inter-Generational Youth Ministry: Why a Balanced View of Connecting the Generations is Essential for the Church*, which is available at: https://www.youthministryquestions.com/book-store/inter-generational-youth-ministry.

5. **Youth ministry is turning to real ministry and not merely programming.**

There has been a resurgence of interest in involving teenagers in ministry on a regular basis in their home churches, and not just when they are away from home on their annual mission trip. Many youth workers are now working hard to help their young people discover and use their spiritual gifts in various ministry capacities, which includes active exposure to other age groups, in their home churches.

Youth ministry is indeed at a crossroads. It's time to make sure that our youth ministries are built on a solid biblical and theological foundation.

Our youth ministry forefathers taught us how to look at cultural trends as a conduit for innovative programs and methods. We can learn from that, but let's make sure that the Scriptures are the basis for what we do and how we do it.

This article first appeared: https://www.youthpastortheologian.com/blog/historical-and-theological-trends-in-youth-ministry.

CHAPTER 34

HOW CAN YOU LAST IN YOUTH MINISTRY OVER THE LONG HAUL?

LET ME INTRODUCE YOU TO two of my heroes.

The first was my Sunday School teacher when I was in junior high. I thought he was too old, too strict, and way too conservative to work with students. I hate to admit it now, but I'd complain about him to my dad. Come to find out, he was also my dad's Sunday School teacher at that age. This faithful leader served the junior high youth group in my home church for over 30 years! He's in Heaven now, but you'll meet him there someday. He'll be in the front row - after working with early adolescents for that long (with guys like me in his group), he deserves to be in the front row!

The second was a youth worker that I've known for over 45 years. He served for almost 25 years as a youth pastor in two local churches and coached in public high schools for over 20 years. He still leads an international youth ministry organization, and he travels to speak to hundreds of kids each year in camps, retreats, and other youth events.

The bottom line is that he is a youth worker, and I can't picture him doing anything else.

I've told churches for years that people may get too old to play tackle football (I would probably fall on you and crush you), but you never get too old to minister to kids!

So, what are the keys to longevity in student ministry?

1. **What has God called, gifted, and equipped you to do?**

   It's really quite simple: if God has called you and blessed you with the ability to work with students, then do it, and keep doing it for as long as you can. Honestly, why would you stoop to do anything else?

2. **Do you love students?**

   If the Lord has put a burden on your heart for middle schoolers, high schoolers, or even young adults, then I believe that you'll do anything you can to spend time with them and their families to reach them for Christ and to help them to go on for Him. It's not just a cliché; youth workers work with youth, and they keep working with youth.

3. **Are you willing to be a servant?**

   Let's face it, sometimes ministry is hard, and it takes faithfulness over the long haul. Kids need adults to be faithful, to be the kind of people they can depend upon. You may want to resign every Monday morning, but don't do it! Teenagers need loving, caring, and faithful adults to be an ongoing part of their lives.

4. **How can you make the greatest impact for eternity?**

Reproducing yourself in the lives of the next generation may be the most important characteristic of a true leader. As I write this post, I am reminded that there is one real advantage to getting old in youth ministry. You stay around enough to see the students that you invested your life in grow up and go on for God. That scenario is an incredible blessing.

5. **How can you change and adapt to stay effective?**

Unless God has other plans, all of us will get older. But we don't have to act old. Young people may laugh at our choice of clothes or our taste in music. But even older youth workers can have an incredible impact on the lives of kids just by caring enough to stay faithful to our calling. Sure, we need to change and adapt our methodologies, and work hard to stay current and relevant. But that doesn't mean that we put on an act in a misguided attempt to look young or "hip". That's a slippery slope. Today's young people are looking for adult youth workers who genuinely care enough to be involved in their lives. It doesn't matter how old we are. It does matter that we care about kids and demonstrate our unconditional love for them.

Older people can be very effective youth workers. The above listed ideas may help develop longevity in youth ministry. To quote a song by the old crooner, Steve Green, I hope that the generations to come will "find us faithful!"[1]

ENDNOTES

Chapter 1

[1] "The Top Reasons Young People Drop Out of Church". Griffon Jackson, Christianity Today. 2019.

[2] For example: "Biblical Youth Ministry", Scott Brown. scottbrownonline.com, 2013

[3] "What is the Shema?" Tim Mackie, BibleProject, 2019.

[4] *A Biblical Theology of Youth Ministry: Teenagers in the Lord of the Church*, Michael McGarry, published by Randall House Publications, 2019, pages 19-20.

Chapter 2

[1] *Essential Church? Reclaiming a Generation of Dropouts*, Thom Rainer and Sam Rainer, published by B&H Books, 2008, page 3.

[2] *The Rise of the Nones, Understanding And Reaching The Religiously Unaffiliated*, James Emery White, published by Baker Books, 2014.

[3] *Contagious Faith: Empowering Student Leadership in Youth Evangelism*, Dave Rahn & Terry Linhart, published by Group Publishing, 2000, p. 19.

[4] "Are Short-Term Missions Good Stewardship?" Robert Priest, Kurt Ver Beek. Christianity Today, 2005.

[5] *Contagious Faith: Empowering Student Leadership in Youth Evangelism*, p. 19

[6] Dewey Bertoloni at the National Youth Ministries Conference.

Chapter 3

1   For example: "Most Teenagers Drop Out of Church When They Become Young Adults". Lifeway Research, 2019.

2   "Interview with Dr. 'Chap' Clark". The Christian Post, 2005.

Chapter 6

1   http://www.oxymoronlist.com/

Chapter 7

1   "When did Sunday Schools start?" Timothy Larson, Christianity Today, 2008.

Chapter 9

1   https://joshuaproject.net/

2   "Why is Gen Z called Gen Z?" Flashmode, 2021.

3   "Meet Generation Alpha". Khumo Theko, Flux Trends.

4   *Generation Z: A Century in the Making*, Corey Seemiller and Meghan Grace, published by Routledge, 2019, pages 39-55.

5   *Households of Faith: The Rituals and Relationships That Turn a Home Into a Sacred Space*, edited by the Barna Group, published by Barna Group, 2019, page 22.

6   *Youth Ministry in a Post-Christian World*, by Brock Morgan, published by The Youth Cartel, LLC, 2013, pages 20-37.

7   *The Post-Church Christian: Dealing with the Generational Baggage of Our Faith*, by J. Paul Nyquist and Carson Nyquist, published by Moody Publishers, 2013, pages 11-15.

8   *iGen: Why Today's Super-Connected Kids are Growing Up Less Rebellious, More Tolerant, Less Happy – and Completely Unprepared for Adulthood and What That Means for the Rest of Us*, by Jean M. Twenge, published by Atria (Simon & Schuster, Inc.), 2017, page, 10.

9   "Baby Bust: Explaining The Declining US Birth Rate." 1A, NPR. 2021.

10   "US population by generation." Statista, 2021.

11 "The Complete Guide To Generation Alpha, The Children Of Millennials." Christine Carter, Forbes. 2016.

12 "The Rise of Post-Familialism: Humanity's Future?" Joel Kotkin, Newgeography.com, 2012.

13 "The Church of Laodicea in the Bible and Archaeology". Megan Sauter, Biblical Archaeology Society, 2021.

14 A phrase first coined by Dr. Christian Smith in *Soul Searching: The Religious and Spiritual Lives of American Teenagers* published by Oxford University Press, 2005, citing the results of the "National Study of Youth & Religion".

15 *Meet Generation Z: Understanding and Reaching the New Post-Christian World,* by James Emery White, published by Baker Books, 2017, pages 107-128.

Chapter 10

1 *Generation Z: A Century in the Making,* by Corey Seemiller and Meghan Grace, published by Routledge, 2018.

2 "Generation Z Statistics". Vision Critical Blog.

3 "Spearheading Change at the Speed of Culture, Gen Z Are the Final Generation." Slideshare, 2015.

4 "Top 10 Things to Consider As You START Doing Generation Z Ministry." Dan Istvanik, YS Blog. 2017.

5 *Faith for Exiles: 5 Ways for a New Generation to Follow Jesus in Digital Babylon,* by David Kinnaman and Mark Matlock, published by Baker Books, 2019.

6 *Meet Generation Z: Understanding and Reaching the New Post-Christian World,* by James Emery White, p.131.

7 Households of Faith: The Rituals and Relationships That Turn a Home Into a Sacred Space by Barna Group, 2019.

8 *Generation Z: A Century in the Making,* by Corey Seemiller and Meghan Grace.

9 *Faith for Exiles: 5 Ways for a New Generation to Follow Jesus in Digital Babylon,* by David Kinnaman and Mark Matlock.

10 "The State of the Church 2016". Barna Group, 2016.

11 *The Rise of the Nones, Understanding And Reaching The Religiously Unaffiliated,* James Emery White.

Chapter 11

[1] *When God Shows Up: A History of Protestant Youth Ministry in America*, Mark H. Senter III, published by Baker Academic, Grand Rapids, MI, 2010.

[2] https://generationalpha.com/

[3] "Evangelism Is Most Effective Among Kids." Barna Group, 2004.

[4] "5 Big Ideas For Ministry To Increasingly Dysfunctional Households". Mel Walker, YS Blog. 2020.

Chapter 12

[1] "Interview with Dr. 'Chap' Clark". The Christian Post, 2005.

Chapter 13

[1] *Future Shock*, Alvin Toffler, published by Random House, Inc. (reprinted in 1990 by Bantam Books), 1970.

[2] *Generation Z: A Century in the Making*, by Corey Seemiller and Meghan Grace, published by Routlegde, 2018.

[3] "The Rise of Post-Familialism: Humanity's Future?" Joel Kotkin, Newgeography.com, 2012.

[4] "Households of Faith: The Rituals and Relationships That Turn a Home Into a Sacred Space." Barna Group, 2019.

[5] "Nuclear Family or Church Family? Yes." Harriet Connor, Gospel Coalition, 2015.

[6] See Chapter 18 in this book for more information on "spiritual orphans."

[7] For more information on church-based mentoring see my book, *Mentoring the Next Generation: A Practical Strategy for Connecting the Generations in Your Church.*

Chapter 16

[1] "New Children's Ministry Statistics: How do kids come to Christ?" Tony Kummer, Ministry-to-Children, 2020.

[2] "Why is it Called the Nuclear Family?" Merriam-Webster.

Chapter 17

1 "When Americans Become Christians." National Association of Evangelicals.

2 A great resource on the current state of the family in the US is *Households of Faith*, by Barna Research.

3 I recently wrote a post on my blog about building safeguards into our mentoring ministry. Check it out here: http://melwalker.org/mentoring-safeguards/

4 See *Mentoring the Next Generation: A Practical Strategy for Connecting the Generations in Your Church*, by Mel Walker, published by Vision For Youth Publishing, 2019. https://goingonforgod.com/product/mentoring/

5 See *Inter-Generational Youth Ministry: Why A Balanced View of Connecting the Generations is Essential for the Church*, by Mel Walker, published by Vision For Youth Publishing, 2013. http://intergenerationalyouthministry.com/the-book/

6 See *Going On For God: Encouraging the Next Generation to Grow Up and Go On For God*, by Mel Walker, published by Vision For Youth Publishing, 2108. https://goingonforgod.com/product/going-on-for-god/

Chapter 20

1 From a message presented at Vision For Youth's National Youth Ministries Conference.

2 Also taken from a message presented at Vision for Youth's National Youth Ministries Conference.

3 "Who Is Responsible for Children's Faith Formation?" Barna Group, 2019.

4 *Family Based Youth Ministry*, by Mark DeVries, published by Inter-Varsity Press, p. 177.

Chapter 28

1 "Inside the Teen Brain...". Walt Mueller, CPYU, 2013.

2 *A Parent's Guide to Understanding Teenage Brains: Why They Act the Way They Do*, by Mark Oestreicher, published by Simply Youth Ministry, 2012.

3 "5 Reasons Millennials Stay Connected to Church", Barna Group, 2013; and "Moving Away from the Kid Table", Kara Powell, Fuller Youth Institute, 2010.

Chapter 31

[1] "What Two Simple Statistics Reveal about the American Church." Sam Rainer, samrainer.com, 2016.

[2] "More teens addicted to social media, prefer texting to talking". Erika Edwards, Maggie Fox. NBC News, 2018.

Chapter 32

[1] Note: I understand that NASCAR historically has held 2 races each year at Pocono Raceway, but according to recent news reports they have decided to trim that number down to only one race.

Chapter 34

[1] "Find Us Faithful." Steve Green, Sparrow Records, 1988.

BIBLIOGRAPHY

A Biblical Theology of Youth Ministry: Teenagers in the Lord of the Church, Michael McGarry, published by Randall House Publications, 2019.

Contagious Faith: Empowering Student Leadership in Youth Evangelism, Dave Rahn and Terry Linhart, published by Group Publishing, 2000.

Essential Church? Reclaiming a Generation of Dropouts, Thom Rainer and Sam Rainer, published by B&H Books, 2008.

Faith for Exiles: 5 Ways for a New Generation to Follow Jesus in Digital Babylon, by David Kinnaman and Mark Matlock, published by Baker Books, 2019.

Family Based Youth Ministry, by Mark DeVries, published by Inter-Varsity Press, 2004.

Future Shock, Alvin Toffler, published by Random House, Inc. (reprinted in 1990 by Bantam Books), 1970.

Generation Z: A Century in the Making, Corey Seemiller and Meghan Grace, published by Routledge, 2019.

iGen: Why Today's Super-Connected Kids are Growing Up Less Rebellious, More Tolerant, Less Happy – and Completely Unprepared for Adulthood and

What That Means for the Rest of Us, by Jean M. Twenge, published by Atria (Simon & Schuster, Inc.), 2017.

Meet Generation Z: Understanding and Reaching the New Post-Christian World, by James Emery White, published by Baker Books, 2017.

A Parent's Guide to Understanding Teenage Brains: Why They Act the Way They Do, by Mark Oestreicher, published by Simply Youth Ministry, 2012.

The Post-Church Christian: Dealing with the Generational Baggage of Our Faith, by J. Paul Nyquist and Carson Nyquist, published by Moody Publishers, 2013.

The Rise of the Nones, Understanding And Reaching The Religiously Unaffiliated, James Emery White, published by Baker Books, 2014.

When God Shows Up: A History of Protestant Youth Ministry in America, Mark H. Senter III, published by Baker Academic, Grand Rapids, MI, 2010.

Youth Ministry in a Post-Christian World, by Brock Morgan, published by The Youth Cartel, LLC, 2013.

ABOUT MEL

Mel Walker was the president and co-founder of Vision For Youth, Inc., an international network for youth ministry. In his lifetime, Mel was a frequent speaker (both nationally and internationally) at youth, church leadership, family life, and parenting conferences. He spoke to thousands of students, church leaders, and youth workers each year and organized and led several regional, statewide, and national youth and youth ministry conferences and events.

Mel graduated from Clarks Summit University (then Baptist Bible College and Seminary) with his AA, BRE, and M. Min, and completed graduate work at Iowa State University and Faith Baptist Theological Seminary. Mel and his wife, Peggy, have three grown children, and now have 10 grandchildren.

Mel began his career ministry as a youth pastor in Michigan, then taught youth and family ministry courses and served in various administrative roles at Faith Baptist Bible College in Ankeny, Iowa, and then at Baptist Bible College and Seminary in Clarks Summit, PA. He also ministered for several years as the director of student ministries at a denominational publishing company – where he led in their complete revision of the youth ministry curriculum. Before his full time ministry through Vision For Youth, Mel served as youth pastor and assistant pastor at Wyoming Valley Church in Wilkes-Barre, PA.

He was the author of 13 other books, including *Inter-Generational Youth Ministry: Why a Balanced View of Connecting the Generations is Essential for the Church,* and *Going On For God: Encouraging the Next Generation to Grow Up & Go On For God.*

Mel passed away on December 2, 2021, shortly before the publication of this, his final book. Thank you for taking the time to read his last written words. His other books are available online at <u>www. youthministryquestions.com</u>.

Going On For God: Encouraging the Next Generation to Grow Up and Go On For God

$15.99 / paperback

$7.99 / PDF

"'What Do We Want For Our Kids?' If you are a Christian parent or grandparent, of if you are a pastor, youth pastor, or other church leader, I think you would agree that we want our kids to grow up and on for God as adults. Right?

Youth ministry should never be a terminal program where teenagers graduate from high school, finish their involvement in youth group, and then walk away from the church. Yet that is what is happening in the lives of so many emerging adults. It is time to stop the exodus of young adults walking away from God.

This book is a practical conversation for Christian parents and church leaders who are interested in proactive suggestions for encouraging the next generation to grow up spiritually and to live their adults lives as devoted followers of Christ. This process isn't easy, but take it from someone who has been a fellow-struggler on this journey – it's certainly worth the effort. We are in this together as part of God's Word in the world today. We want our kids to grow up and go on for God!"

Going On For God – Study Guide to Help Christian Parents AND Church Leaders be a Part of This Important Conversation

$5.00 / paperback

$4.00 / PDF

It is my goal to make this study guide to my book, Going On For God: Encouraging the Next Generation to Grow Up and Go On For God, both as Biblically based and as practical as possible. My prayer is that it can be utilized in your church as a catalyst for a growing conversation between Christian parents and church leaders (pastors, youth pastors, volunteers, youth leaders, teachers, and children's workers), to help them discuss together the critically-important topic of encouraging the next generation to grow up and go on for God. And isn't that what we want for our kids?

Inter-Generational Youth Ministry: Why a Balanced View of Connecting the Generations is Essential for the Church

$12.00 / paperback

$7.99 / PDF

It's time to bridge the generation gap in the church. For too long, traditional churches have isolated the various generations from each other. This segregation has resulted in a mass exodus from the church following active participation in youth ministry. It's time to reverse that trend by taking proactive steps to connect the generations the church without destroying the many positive aspects of church youth ministry.

Convinced. Applying Biblical Principles to Life's Choices

$9.99 / paperback

$6.99 / PDF

How do we know what God wants us to do?

We are living in a culture with very few absolutes. Moral relativism rules contemporary society. When asked to make a choice on almost any current issue, many of today's young people will respond by saying, "It depends." So many are struggling with knowing right from wrong.

That's why this devotional booklet, that my kids and I put together, is so important. God's Word has clear and uncompromising reasons for decision making. As you work your way through the thirty daily devotionals, notice the Bible's use of words like: all, every, always, and everything.

In one month, as you seek to apply these 30 Biblical principles, you will be able to develop your own Biblical convictions for life's issues. Whatever the issue, the Bible has answers.

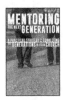

Mentoring the Next Generation: A Practical Strategy for Connecting the Generations in Your Church

$12.99 / paperback

$7.99 / PDF

"Mentoring is a way for local churches to make intentional and growing, inter-generational connections. I define mentoring as the practice of caring and Godly, older adults taking the initiative to develop personal, growing relationships with younger people to encourage spiritual and personal maturity.

This can be an incredibly practical way to build God-honoring connections in your church. Even today's busy adults can mentor eager young people by utilizing activities that are already a part of their schedules to build these connections. Effective mentoring can happen in the church foyer, on a golf course, or in a crowded coffee shop. It can take place while running errands or while serving together in the church.

This easy-to-read and easy-to-apply book provides a real-world and pro-active strategy to practically connect the generations in your church."

Pushing the Limits: Unleashing the Potential of Student Ministry

$5.00 / hardback

In this book, I join with veteran youth worker, Mike Calhoun, to collect some of the best input from youth pastors and leaders all around the country, who are doing what it takes to tap into the true potential of youth ministry. Readers will find each of the chapters in this classic anthology to have been written by experienced practitioners – some from smaller churches, others from large churches, and others who are knowledgeable youth ministry specialists. Each writer has a clear-cut passion to effectively communicate the truth of God's Word to a needy generation.